Unforgotten
Dreams

Translations from the Asian Classics

Unforgotten Dreams

POEMS BY
THE ZEN MONK
SHŌTETSU

EDITED AND TRANSLATED BY
Steven D. Carter

NEW YORK ✦ COLUMBIA UNIVERSITY PRESS

Columbia University Press
Publishers Since 1893
New York   Chichester, West Sussex

Copyright © 1997 Columbia University Press

All rights reserved

Columbia University Press wishes to express its appreciation of assistance given by the Pushkin Fund in the publication of this translation.

Library of Congress Cataloging-in-Publication Data

Shōtetsu, 1381?–1459?

[Poems. English. Selections]

Unforgotten dreams : poems by the Zen monk Shōtetsu /

translated, with an introduction by Steven D. Carter.

p.   cm. — (Translations from the Asian classics)

Includes index.

ISBN 0-231-10576-2. — ISBN 0-231-10577-0 (pbk.)

1. Shōtetsu, 1381?–1459?—Translations into English. 2. Waka—
Translations into English.   I. Carter, Steven D.   II. Title.
III. Series.

PL792.S55A23   1996

895.6'124—dc20

96-21002

CIP

Casebound editions of Columbia University Press books are printed on permanent and durable acid-free paper.

Designed by Linda Secondari

Printed in the Uniteed States of America

c 10 9 8 7 6 5 4 3 2 1

p 10 9 8 7 6 5 4 3 2 1

to Mary

CONTENTS

ACKNOWLEDGMENTS

For constant support and encouragement I thank my wife Mary, to whom this book is dedicated. Thanks also are due to two anonymous readers for Columbia University Press, who made useful suggestions for improvement of the manuscript, and to my editor, Jennifer Crewe.

*Unforgotten
Dreams*

The annals of Japanese literary history abound with stories of suffering literati. First among these, of course, is the case of Sugawara no Michizane (845–903), the famous court minister who after being slandered by competitors was exiled to Dazaifu, where legend says he quite literally died of grief. Then there is the story of the early eleventh-century poet Fujiwara no Nagatō, who responded to the criticism of a powerful contemporary by withdrawing to his house and starving himself to death. Lastly, one recalls the tale of the medieval poet Keiun (fl. 1340–1370), an unhappy man who became so distressed at his failure to find praise as a poet that just before death he destroyed all of his poems in an attempt to deny posterity the opportunity to gloat.

None of these, however, seems to have borne more grief than the Zen monk Shōtetsu (1381–1459), the author of the poems translated in this book. For Shōtetsu was not once but thrice stricken: first, by the loss of all of the poems of his first thirty years—more than 30,000 of them—in a fire that destroyed his residence in 1432, at the age of fifty-two; second, by the confiscation of his estate revenues by an angry shogun at around the same time; and lastly by the refusal of his rivals to allow him any representation whatsoever in the only imperially commissioned poetic anthology of his time, the *Shin shokuko-kinshū* of 1439.

But a closer look at the record of Shōtetsu's life reveals that his misfortunes did not defeat him. Indeed, by all standards save the one of representation in an imperial anthology, he was a successful poet, which is to say not only that he was able to make a living from his literary practice but that in the process of doing so he won recognition from some quarters as a true master of his art and left behind a large body of work. By his time, the Way of the classical *uta*—the name given to the thirty-one syllable form that was Shōtetsu's chosen genre—was already more than seven centuries old and seemingly beyond its prime. Nonetheless, the form was still the most prestigious of genres, and still occupied a central place in the the literary culture of the noble houses and the military aristocracy, both in the capital city of Kyoto and in the numerous "little" Kyotos of the provinces. Notwithstanding the many literary histories that refer to the time as the age of linked verse (*renga*), it was the *uta* and its aesthetic traditions that dominated literary discourse.

It was into this literary situation that Shōtetsu was born in 1381. Although no historical record says anything about his childhood, remarks he made to disciples in later years reveal that he began his walk on the Way quite conventionally when his father, a samurai of middling rank named Komatsu Yasukiyo, brought him and the rest of the family to Kyoto in the 1390s. Evidently to discourage the teenager, formally named Masakiyo but known casually as Sonmyōmaru at the time, from pursuing a literary career, his father put him in a temple in Nara soon thereafter. Since temples were centers of learning that often provided entrance into various artistic professions for talented commoners, however, the plan backfired: for it was evidently while pursuing the Way of Buddha that Shōtetsu chose to travel the Way of Poetry—two paths that were not seen by all as incompatible, or, more accurately, as no more incompatible than many others. When his father died, he therefore moved back to the capital, where he continued his religious studies but also his plans to become a professional poet. It comes as no surprise, then, to learn that in 1414 the young poet took vows as a Zen monk named variously Shōtetsu and/or Shōgetsu, serving for a time thereafter as a scribe at Tōfukuji, a large temple located on the southeastern fringes of Kyoto. All of his life he would consider himself a monk, although one for whom poetry was both profession and religious avocation.

Since the late thirteenth century, any commoner hoping to enter practice as a professional poet—by which I mean a poet who made his living primarily from his artistic activities—had been obliged to study under a recognized master who could claim authority through some affiliation with the heirs of the so-called "father" of medieval poetry, Fujiwara no Teika (1162–1241). This Shōtetsu did, under Teika's heir-by-blood the courtier Reizei Tamemasa (1361–1417) and also the warrior literatus Imagawa Ryōshun (1326–1417), two bastions of the more liberal of the poetic factions at court who catechized their promising pupil in the esoteric teachings of their "sect" and supervised his *keiko*, or composition practice. What connections brought Shōtetsu to his teachers is not known, but meeting them was perhaps the most fortunate event of his life, enough, one might even say, to compensate for the disasters that would befall him later. For Tamemasa was a man of rare talent and genuine artistic commitment who, had he not died in 1417, just when he had gained the political power necessary for success at court, might have had a salutary effect on the composition of poetry even in that most conservative of venues; and Ryōshun, although a less-talented poet, was a teacher who stressed creativity and inspired in Shōtetsu the confidence to challenge prevailing conventions.

With such men as supporters and his own native talent, the young man progressed rapidly, making a name for himself in Kyoto by around 1415. Even after his teachers died, he continued to draw on the "symbolic capital" of his affiliation with them and remained on good terms with their heirs. Living first in one cottage in the Rokkaku area of the capital and then in another in Imakumano, he was now a master of the art himself, with a growing number of students. Records make it clear that by this time he was participating frequently in poetic gatherings in the military houses, which constituted the most available market for one of his social status. Specifically, he served as a kind of master at monthly poetry meetings (*tsukinamikai*), poem contests, and votive sequences—three of the most basic forms of communal composition at the time. Such events were in a real sense competitions in which poets tested their competence in a group setting, composing poems on prescribed *dai*, or topics, according to ancient standards and conventions.[1] Here Shōtetsu showed himself a true master, attracting praise and securing an income over and above the estate revenues he seems to have received as a stipend from his family. In this way he was able to rub shoulders with not only some of the most politically mighty men in the capital, but also with other potential students and patrons among their vassals.

However, as a commoner with no hope of gaining formal status in the court hierarchy, Shōtetsu had to leave continuation of the liberal tradition among the nobility to Reizei Tamemasa's heirs by birth. These were not easy times for the Reizei family at court, where their conservative rivals, particularly those in the Asukai family, had the support of the shogun, Ashikaga Yoshinori (1394–1441). It was in fact in this political context that Shōtetsu suffered the loss of his estate revenues and was denied representation in the imperial anthology of 1439—things that might not have happened had Tamemasa still been alive. By this time, however, Shōtetsu was nearly sixty and had suffered enough hardships to be able to maintain hope even under extreme duress. His dedication to the Way of Poetry never wavered; nor were the criticisms of rivals enough to keep him from its practice. And after the death in 1441 of Ashikaga Yoshinori, he was able to gain some prominence even in the salons of the high nobility, particularly the Reizei family and the Regent-literatus Ichijō Kaneyoshi (1402–1481).

Shōtetsu's last fifteen years were therefore prosperous ones, during which he served as master in monthly and other gatherings at the homes of prominent members of the warrior classes and at a number of different temples. During the year 1451, for example, his personal anthology reveals that in addition to participating in poetic activities with courtiers such as Asukai Masachika (1417–1490) and Reizei Mochitame (1401–1454) and fellow professionals such as Gyōkō (1391–1455) and Ninzei (fl. ca. 1440–50), he performed as a master in monthly meetings for the prominent warriors Hatakeyama Yoshitada (d. 1463; also known by his monkish name Kenryō) fifteen times, for Hosokawa Katsumoto (1430–1473) ten times, for Yamana Noriyuki (d. 1473) eight times, and less frequently for Isshiki Norichika (d. 1451), Hosokawa Dōken (d. 1468), Ogasawara Mochinaga (fl. ca. 1430–40), and numerous others—and this in a year when he spent a full two months in Nara during the spring, where he of course participated in numerous other such events while enjoying the seasonal delights at various shrines and temples. In such esteem was he held by Hatakeyama Yoshitada that the warrior even came to visit the poet at his hut when the latter was bedridden with asthma in the Eighth Month, an honor to which Shōtetsu replied by producing thirty poems "while reclining." For that entire year Shōtetsu records in his personal anthology 558 of his poems, composed for at least 108 different events, which judging from internal evidence we may estimate to be only a fraction of the work he actually produced during that same period. Needless to say, he must have been paid for his services, the offering of which demanded not only knowledge and technical virtuosity but also social skills.

Despite his popularity, the effects of Shōtetsu's earlier troubles remained apparent in the boldness with which he stated his dissatisfaction with the petty squabbles of his contemporaries in the noble houses, liberal and conservative alike. For both, according to him, had strayed from the way of the forementioned founder of the late medieval poetic tradition, Teika, for whom Shōtetsu avowed an allegiance verging on worship. "I will be a member of the Teika sect," he told friends, "until I die."[2] Elsewhere he is less cryptic:

It is my opinion that a person should pay no attention whatever to these schools. Instead, he ought to cherish the style and spirit of Teika and strive to emulate him even though he may never succeed. Some will say that this is the path of perfection to which the ordinary mind cannot hope to aspire, and that instead a person should take as his standard the poetic styles of Teika's descendants. However, as the saying goes, 'Emulate the highest art to achieve the mediocre.' So, even if a person cannot attain to it, he should still emulate the highest artistic standard, for then even in failure he may still achieve something of reasonable quality.[3]

To praise Teika was of course nothing revolutionary. All poets of the day, of every lineage and persuasion, recognized Teika as the ultimate authority in poetic matters. But to Shōtetsu their picture of Teika was like a portrait whose original colors and contours had been obscured by the dust of many generations. What he seems to have wanted was the vivid image underneath the dusky pall—a naive wish, one may say, but one that has provided the motivation for many artists before and since.

Shōtetsu's poetic practice, of course, could not be like that of Teika, who had been not a commoner but a courtier living in an age when the court was still a prosperous institution—a situation not at all similar to that of a low-ranking Zen monk who spent most of his time in his own cottage with students or in the meeting halls of warrior patrons. But Shōtetsu believed that poetry was a transcendent medium, and that in his own poetry he could emulate Teika as well as anyone. Thus he set out, particularly in his last years, to produce a body of work worthy at least of comparison with that of his mentor, with the following note of caution as his guide:

> . . . to speak of emulating the style of the Master and then merely to imitate his diction and cadences would be deplorable. Instead, one should constantly emulate his style and spirit and cast of mind.[4]

Whether or not Shōtetsu succeeded in his aims is a matter for readers to decide; but the evidence of his personal anthology, *Sōkonshū* ("Grass Roots"), is enough to prove that he was at least valiant in the attempt. Containing just over 11,000 poems, it is the single largest personal anthology in the classical canon—more than twice as large as Teika's own. As might be expected, not all of the poems are up to his mentor's standards. And since the work as we have it today was put in its final form by disciples after his death, we may even surmise that some of them he would not have wanted anyone else to see. But the great quantity of his work shows us two things: first, that for him composing poetry was, as Marvin Bell says of a modern poet, "sometimes ... like practice" or something "written as an exercise"[5] and, second, that he sought to be a master of all the styles of the tradition, from the style of "intense feeling" (*ushin*) favored by the conservatives of his own day, to the more demanding styles of "mystery and depth" (*yūgen*) and "objective realism" (*ari no mama*) of the Reizei school. In this scholars note the continuing influence of his Reizei teachers, who stressed the importance of discipline and held to the belief that "to tend toward only one style was to constrict the Way."[6] No doubt Shōtetsu himself would claim Teika and not any later poet as his inspiration.

Whatever the case, the important fact for readers is that in *Sōkonshū* one finds poems as dissimilar as these, the first bold in its metaphoric treatment of the confused mental state of one who clings to hope for a lover's note that may mean, figuratively, either life or death, the second—an example of straightforward description—bold only in its simplicity. Here, as in the rest of the translations in this book, I give the prescribed topic (*dai*) of the poem in quotation marks before the poem itself, as a way to emphasize that the topic is not a "title" attached after the fact but rather the "question" to which the poet has been asked to provide an appropriate answer. In the first case, the poem was composed for a hundred-poem sequence for which the topics had been chosen beforehand, and probably not by the poet himself; a similar situation may also have held for the second poem, although it carries no headnote specifying the circumstances of its composition.

"The Unbearable Wait for Love"

Past and
          gone now
is the time I awaited,
leaving me
              clinging—
anxious for wind
                    from the pines,
like dewdrops
              at break of day.[7]

"An Animal, in Spring"

The gloom of dusk.
An ox
        from out
                  in the fields
comes walking my way;
and along
            the hazy road
I encounter
              no one.[8]

Both these poems are conventional in the broad sense of adhering to courtly standards of diction, prosody, and so on. Beyond that, they are so different that one might assume they are by different poets—or perhaps by Teika, whose works reveal a similar range of style.

But there is another major influence at work in Shōtetsu's poems, and it is one that sets him slightly apart from his mentor. That influence is Buddhism, particularly Zen Buddhism. He was a Zen monk by training, after all, who was often refered to by contemporaries as Shōtetsu *zenshi*, or Zen Master; and he says quite explicitly that he hears the Law even in silent things:

"Buddhism: Blossoms"

With every
           new spring
the blossoms
           speak not a word,
yet expound
           the Law—
knowing
           what is at its heart
from the scattering
           storm winds.[9]

One may of course choose to see such poems as no more than conventional statements of the doctrine of mutability (*mujō*), which is so central to the entire medieval poetic tradition. And because his poems tended to be composed in secular settings on preestablished courtly themes rather than in his own chambers as an explicit part of his religious devotions, they are seldom as dogmatic as those of who may be called true "Zen" poets, such as Musō Soseki (1275–1351) or Shōtetsu's own contemporary, Ikkyū Sōjun (1394–1481). But no one reading through *Sōkonshū* can help but be struck by the frequency with which Zen conceptions appear as themes or subthemes in Shōtetsu's poems, regardless of their overt subject matter. In particular, one finds an attitude that rejoices in the quotidian, a tendency to problematize fundamental cognitive categories such as time and consciousness, and an awareness of not just the mutability but also of the transmutability of all things—in the way in time one thing becomes another, merges with another, supplements another, in an endless procession for which the poet acts as a kind of artistic amanuensis:

✓   *"Love—Bell"*

As I listen,
                bells
tolling over Hatsu River
fade off,
            one by one—
falling onto
                my sleeves,
becoming
        the capital.[10]

Clearly, this poem evokes an earlier love poem by Teika, written from the perspective of one who after years of praying has all but given up hope of ever meeting the one yearned for:

> The years
>   have gone by,
>   with my prayers
>   still unanswered—
>   as Hase's bell
>   signals evening
>   from its peak,
>   sounding somehow
>   far away.[11]

Teika's poem, however, is "realistic" when compared to Shōtetsu's, and contains no trace of the Buddhist idea of bell sounds "becoming" first the tears of the lonely speaker and then the very capital itself. In this, Shōtetsu shows himself to be a true cohort of a whole host of other Buddhist artists of his own century, including most conspicuously Zeami (1363–1443), Zenchiku (1405–1468?), and Sesshū (1420–1506), as well as of the Gozan poets who are generally not compared to him only because they wrote their poems in Chinese rather than in Japanese.

However much he may have wanted to transcend it, Shōtetsu was thus in some ways a man of his own time and place. Although more liberal than many of his contemporaries in his views on some matters, he was still a master in the conventional sense, and was certainly no revolutionary out to create a new Way. Rather, he sought to turn the way back toward its founders, whom he judged to be more appropriate models than the court poets of his own epoch. In this political project he failed. Happily, though, his political failure did not deter him from writing poems that do transcend time in the sense that they still resonate for us now, in a time when, as Theodor Adorno succinctly puts it, "absolute contingency . . . is itself the essential."[12]

Shōtetsu died in 1459, before the degradations of the Onin War (1467–77) and other events brought an end to the court society that had been the ultimate provider of both ideological foundation and social sustenance for his genre. Like many other *uta* poets of his day, he was forgotten. Not being represented in any of the imperial anthologies meant that even the restorationist scholars of the Edo period found him easy to overlook. That his name survived at all in narrative histories of Japanese literature was because several of his disciples became major figures in the development of linked-verse, or *renga*, a form for which he seems to have had little sympathy. Thanks to the work of several scholars,[13] however, he has gained a good deal of attention in Japan over the last several decades. My hope is that the translations offered here will serve to encourage more interest in him among English readers, who will then find in his work a mastery that goes beyond the mastery of convention—indeed, to borrow the words of Donald Justice and Robert Mezey describing the neglected poet Henri Coulette, "a sense of utter freedom demonstrated within the severest limits."[14]

A Note on the Translations

As readers of traditional Japanese poetry know, the *uta* form "unfolds" not via patterns of meter or rhyme, but instead according to number of syllables per line (or phrase), each poem consisting of five units coordinated according to the pattern 5–7–5–7–7. In the past different translators have created (or adopted) different English formats in order to suggest the forms of the originals, the most common of which may be represented by the following fine translation of one of Shōtetsu's poems by Robert Brower.

> Hesitant to cross,
> Even the clouds feel their way along,
> Searching the dusk—
> Where the steep path over the peaks
> Lies beneath the trackless snow.[15]

In my translations I have chosen not to use this or any other established format for the simple reason that I want to use the "natural resources" of English to better suggest the variety of pauses and stops in the original *uta* form, which is something that it seems to me a uniform format cannot do. The result for me has been a more elastic vehicle—inspired partly by formats used by Octavio Paz and others—that retains the five-line structure of the original poems while at the same time, I hope, revealing at least partially their various stops and starts, patterns of subordination and apposition, and so forth, via punctuation, capitalization, spacing, and a "jogging" of lines that attempts to show where sentences or phrases begin and end. Thus Shōtetsu's poem in my version reads:

> Still hanging back,
> the clouds, too,
>   this evening
> seem to hesitate—
> before
>   the untrodden snow
> of the plank bridge
>   on the peak.

Another decision I have made is to try, whenever possible, to stick to the syllable count of the originals. This choice may seem more difficult to understand, but the reasons behind it are simply put: I feel the need of limitations to work within, or against, in order to create rhythm and tension. Other means could of course serve the same purpose—say, rhyme, or the use of some established English meter. But since one of my goals is to translate Japanese poems in such a way as to make it clear to English readers that they are somehow different from English poems, I believe using the 5–7–5–7–7 pattern might help make the point. Another virtue of using that pattern or any other that employs relatively short lines is that it discourages the temptation to "pad" the translations with interpretive material.

Finally, I have also decided in matters of syntax and word order to try to follow the patterns of the originals, generally if not in every specific case. Most other translators do the same, and for the same reasons, I assume, namely, that they recognize that many *uta*—which are written in what linguists call a left-branching language—literally syntactically "unfold" as they proceed, with what, for lack of a better term, I call a "punch-line" at the end.

So, I have developed a format and a way of reflecting prosody that I think yields interesting results. I hasten to add, however, that although I do believe mine is a rational format the basic principles of which can be learned and put to use, I am not so vain as to suggest that it should be adopted by anyone else. As I said at the beginning, I developed it in order to allow for a more accurate representation of the various structural patterns of the originals. If other translators adopt other measures in order to do the same thing, I support them in their attempts. We need more translations of classical Japanese poetry, not fewer.

In selecting poems for translation I have tried to represent the full range of Shōtetsu's stylistic achievement, taking examples from all available sources and all periods of his career for which we have records. Because it contains more headnotes than other texts, I have used the text of *Sōkonshu* contained in the *Shikashū taisei* series (for bibliographical information on this and other texts, see p. 000), in which the poems are arranged in rough chronological order. My hope is that the headnotes will be of interest to those who want to understand more about the concrete features of poetic practice in Shōtetsu's day, since what the headnotes reveal is that his aesthetic creations emerged almost always from a specific social context—that he was, in this sense, no other-worldly hermit but a man of the world.

ENDNOTES

1. Topics were sometimes given out in advance, sometimes on the spot (*tōza*). For Shōtetsu's attitude toward them, see his comments in *Shōtetsu monogatari*. Robert H. Brower and Steven D. Carter, *Conversations with Shōtetsu* (Ann Arbor: Center for Japanese Studies, 1992).

2. Quoted in *Tōyashū kikigaki*, the memoir of his sometime student Tō no Tsuneyori (1402–84). See vol. 5 of Sasaki Nobutsuna et al., eds., *Nihon kagaku taikei* (Tokyo: Kazama Shobō, 1977), p. 336.

3. See *Conversations with Shōtetsu*, p. 62.

4. Ibid.

5. Bell is paraphrasing the poet William Stafford. See Marvin Bell, *Old Snow Just Melting: Essays and Interviews* (Ann Arbor: University of Michigan Press, 1983), p. 250.

6. *Conversations with Shōtetsu*, p. 10.

7. *Sōkonshū* 9774; poem 185 below. For bibliographical information on Sōkonshū, see p. 209.

8. Sōkonshū 2915; poem 59 below.

9. Sōkonshū 5140; poem 101 below.

10. Sōkonshū 8014; poem 152 below.

11. Poem no. 1142 in *Shin kokinshū*, eighth of the imperially commissioned anthologies of *uta*. For the original, see vol. 1 of Taniyama Shigeru et al., eds., *Shimpen kokka taikan* (Tokyo: Kadokawa Shoten, 1983). The translation is taken from my *Traditional Japanese Poetry: An Anthology* (Stanford: Stanford University Press, 1991), p. 198.

12. Theodor Adorno, *Minima Moralia*, tr. E. F. N. Jephcott (London: Verso, 1974), p. 113.

13. In particular, Inoue Muneo and Inada Toshinori. The latter's *Shōtetsu no kenkyū* (Kasama Shoin, 1978) is now generally accepted as the standard introduction to the poet's life and work.

14. From the Introduction to *The Collected Poems of Henri Coulette* (Fayetteville: University of Arkansas Press, 1991), p. xv.

15. *Conversations with Shōtetsu*, p. 71.

THE POEMS

"Blossoms at Their Height"

Moss
     in the garden
and the blue
        of the sky—
both becoming one;
blossoms
      opening to rise
into white clouds
        of spring.

✦ ✦ ✦ ✦ ✦

niwa no koke / sora no midori mo / hitotsu nite /
hana sakinoboru / haru no shirakumo

2

At dusk I was crossing toward Ōharano when the sky over my path clouded up. Soon lightning flashed, thunder rumbled noisily, wind blew down from the mountains, followed by rain like a summer shower, falling in torrents. Shortly the skies cleared and the evening sun shone brightly, making the cherry blossoms sparkle as if they were so many dewdrops. And all around the evergreens, too, were covered with snowy blossoms that as we walked beneath the trees produced an indescribable effect I had never before seen.

A withering wind
suddenly
    becomes
        a rain shower
and then thunder—
echoes accompanying
        blossoms
as they scatter
    and fall.

✦ ✦ ✦ ✦ ✦

fukishioru / arashi mo ame ni / narukami no /
hibiki o soete / chiru sakura kana

3

On the inkwell stand of the Senior Assistant of the Central Affairs Ministry was this scene: a place where plum blossoms floated on a stream, above which a man stood on top of a bridge, with mountains in the distance and half of the moon visible on the mountain rim. Next to the plum trees Reverend Ishō had inscribed this Chinese poem:

> Walking stick in hand, a man stands on the bridge;
> no wind, yet a scent floats on the dark waters.
> Waves move away, as if resenting something;
> only that lonely shadow refuses to go along.

Above the waves
of life
      in the floating
            world,
the moon hesitates
—coming
       up,
         or going
            down?—
on the rough shore
        of the mountain rim.

✦ ✦ ✦ ✦ ✦

sumigataki / ukiyo o nami no / araiso ni /
izuru ka iru ka / yama no ha no tsuki

4   *"Waterbirds on Pools"*

From afar,
               I see
how peacefully
                    the birds float
on calm waters—
while I am here
                    on thin ice
above
         perilous pools.

✦ ✦ ✦ ✦ ✦

ukitori no / nodoka ni sumu o / yoso ni mite /
ayauki fuchi no / usukōri kana

"Brazier Fire"

If in this world
there were deeds
                mine alone to do—
then I might resent
my name
          being hidden
                  away:
one small coal
          in a box fire.*

♦ ♦ ♦ ♦ ♦

*sashite yo ni / nasu kotowaza no / araba koso /
na o uzumibi no / mi to mo uramime*

Uzumibi, a small coal fire in a brazier.

6

At the shrine in Ninnaji, after the blossoms had already faded and there were few people about, some monks and a lot of other people came and set to drinking beneath the trees. Thoroughly drunk, they took big stones and knocked down all the remaining blossoms, had a good laugh about it, and proceeded to break off some of the lower branches. Since there was no one there to chastise them, I could only look on in dismay. Then I began to wonder what they would think of me and hurried home.

> What right
>   do they have
> to scatter all the blossoms,
> stealing whole branches?
> Like white waves
>   they pass by—
> wanting to be called
>   breakers?*

♦ ♦ ♦ ♦ ♦

*hana o nado / uchichirashite wa / taoruran /
shiranami no na o / tachi ya kasanemu*

---

* The word *shiranami*, "whitecaps" or "breakers," was used metaphorically to refer to thieves.

An old carriage
with its legs near to collapse
stops for a rest—
worn out from traveling far
on
     the way
               of love.

♦ ♦ ♦ ♦ ♦

*furihateshi / ashiyowaguruma / yasurai ni /
yukitsukarenuru / koi no michi kana*

8

Visiting the rooms where Murasaki Shikibu is said to have conceived *The Tale of Genji*, I thought of how only part of that story has come down to us.*

> Here
>   at the place
> from which all
>   once issued forth,
> I draw
>   a few drops—
> thinking
>   how that distant source
> came
>   at last
>   to such an end.

♦ ♦ ♦ ♦ ♦

kore yori mo / nagareshi mizu no / minamoto o /
wazuka ni kumeru / sue o shi zo omou

---

* Medieval legend had it that it was while visiting Ishiyama Temple that Murasaki Shikibu received the initial inspiration for her famous tale. Like most medieval readers, Shōtetsu believed that the work as it existed in his day was missing a final chapter.

"Cicadas on a Late Summer Night"

Off in
      the distance,
the voice
      of a droning
cicada passes;
in the branches,
      all is still
as daylight fades,
      in summer.

✦ ✦ ✦ ✦ ✦

ochikata ni / nakitatsu semi no / koe sugite /
kozue shizuka ni / kururu natsu kana

10   *"Seedlings in the Evening"*

In numbers
                unseen,
planting women
                    sing planting songs
with voices clear—
as the sunlight fades away
where they work
                in seedling beds.

✦ ✦ ✦ ✦ ✦

kazu mienu / ueme no tauta / koe shiruku /
tasogaredoki mo / toru sanae kana

Both noon
            and night
meet here
            in the summertime—
as
    on the pathway
once traversed
            by winter's sun
the moon
        now makes its way.

♦ ♦ ♦ ♦ ♦

*hiru to yoru to / aeru natsu kana / fuyu no hi no /
watarishi michi ni / tsuki ya yukuran*

12   *"Travelers Crossing a Bridge"*

For a few moments
the travelers
                stop speaking
what's on
                their minds:
so narrow
                is the way
across
        an unfamiliar bridge.

♦ ♦ ♦ ♦ ♦

omou koto / shibashi zo iwanu / tabibito no /
watarinarawanu / hashi hosoku shite

"Dream in a Traveler's Inn"

After awaking,
I forgot
      for a moment
I was
      on the road—
still feeling comfortable
in the wake
      of my dream.

✦ ✦ ✦ ✦ ✦

*samete dani / shibashi tabine o / wasururu ya /
minareshi yume no / nagori naruran*

14   *"The Sound of a Waterfall in the Mountains"*

As if
      to conceal
within the folds
          of her robe
a dear wife's tears—
so in the mountain's bosom
descends
      a waterfall.

✦ ✦ ✦ ✦ ✦

wagimoko ga / koromo ni kakusu / namida to ya /
yamafutokoro ni / taki no otsuran

"Along the Path Through a Market"

Along the pathway,
the wind
                of evening
raises
            its voice.
In the market—
                    no one,
only the dust
            piling up.

✦ ✦ ✦ ✦ ✦

michinobe ya / yūbe no kaze no / koe su nari /
ichi ni hito naki / chiri wa tsumorite

16   *"Sunset Over a Woodcutter's Path"*   ✓

Down
      from the peak
came a bundle
        of firewood,
where
      for a moment
I saw light
        from the evening sun—
hauled down
        on a woodsman's back.

✦ ✦ ✦ ✦ ✦

mine kudaru / takigi no ue ni / shibashi mishi /
yūhi no kage o / orosu yamabito

"Rain at a Hut"

Within
      my shelter,
still droplets like jewels
            strike
my soundless sleeves.
Through the rough thatch
            of my eaves—
passing showers
      of moonlight.

✦ ✦ ✦ ✦ ✦

kage nagara / oto naki sode ni / tama zo chiru /
kaya ga nokiba no / tsuki no murasame

18   *"The Gods"*

Besides
        myself
there is
        no other god!
For the gods
            themselves
know that it is
            in men's hearts
that their own gods
                may be found.

♦ ♦ ♦ ♦ ♦

ware naranu / kami koso nakere / kami ya mata /
hito no kokoro o / kami to shiruran

[From a sixty-poem votive sequence commissioned by Hosokawa Dōkan for presentation to Tonshōji in 1414].

> A jeweled missive—
> ink darker here,
> > fainter there,
> scrawled across the page.
> As now
> > both far and near
> wild geese fly off,
> > going home.

♦ ♦ ♦ ♦ ♦

*tamazusa no / kozumi usuzumi / kakitsurane /
ima ochikochi ni / kaeru karigane*

20   *"Fireflies on an Inlet"*

[From a fifty-poem sequence composed in 1416.]

In the dark
                    waves
of an inlet,
                    in the reeds,
they hide themselves;
Are they there?
                    or are they not—
in the shafts of
                    firefly light.

✦ ✦ ✦ ✦ ✦

nami kuraki / irie no ashi ni / migakurete /
aru ka naki ka no / hotarubi no kage

[From a hundred-poem sequence composed as a votive offering to Kitano Shrine in 1420].

> Beneath the cliff,
> the water dripping
>   onto moss
> is hidden by trees—
> but still
>   its sound
>   clears the heart
> of one taking
>   lodging there.

◆ ◆ ◆ ◆ ◆

iwagane no / koke no shizuku mo / kogakurete /
oto ni kokoro o / sumasu yado kana

22   *"Planted Trees"*

[From a hundred-poem sequence composed in one day in 1429].

> Never knowing
> they would
>   remind me
>   of him,
> he planted
>   the trees
> in those days
>   of his
>   old age—
> thinking only of blossoms.

+ + + + +

katami to mo / mimu to mo shirazu / oi ga yo ni /
tada hana nareba / uetekeru kana

23   *"Seedlings"*

[From a single-day hundred-poem sequence composed as a votive offering to the Gion Shrine on the seventh day of the Sixth Month of 1438].

> After a long day
> among
>   seedlings
>   in countless fields,
> they are planted out—
> young maidens
>   resting on paths
> between
>   mountain paddies.

✦ ✦ ✦ ✦ ✦

nagaki hi no / chimachi no sanae / uetsukare /
yamada no kuro ni / yasumu saotome

24   *"Living in Seclusion"*

[From a hundred-poem sequence presented as a votive offering to Sumiyoshi Shrine in 1440].

> Since
> >   no one
> >   visits,
> I have nobody to chat with—
> making
> >   my house
> seem
> >   the kind of place
> >   where lives
> a person
> >   with no cares.

+ + + + +

kataru beki / hito shi towaneba / omou koto /
naki ni mo nitaru / sumika narikeri

"Paddy Hut"

[From a hundred-poem sequence presented as a votive offering to Sumiyoshi Shrine in 1440].

> Those rice plants
> > I saw
> in the gate paddies
> > last autumn—
> were they all
> > a dream?
> Now in the hut
> > made of reeds
> there is no one
> > to spend
> > > the night.*

✦ ✦ ✦ ✦ ✦

aki ni mishi / kadota no inaba / yume nare ya /
ashi no maroya wa / nuru hito mo nashi

---

* Before the harvest, a paddy guard would have been there to protect the crop. An allusive variation on *Shin kokinshū* 625, by Saigyō (1118–90): That spring long ago / at Naniwa in Tsu— / was it all a dream? / Now only dead leaves on the reeds / rustle in the passing wind. (*tsu no kuni no / naniwa no haru wa / yume nare ya / ashi no kareha ni / kaze wataru nari*)

26   *"Lament"*

[From a hundred-poem sequence presented as a votive offering to Sumiyoshi Shrine in 1449].

In this
          world of ours,
what good
             does it do
                   for you
to have
        the praise
                of men?
For blossoms,
             the winds of spring;
for the moon,
             floating clouds.*

✦ ✦ ✦ ✦ ✦

kono yo ni wa / homare aru na mo / nani ka sen /
hana ni harukaze / tsuki ni ukigumo

* Even the fame of things most highly praised, such as blossoms and the moon, can be easily obscured.

"Fireflies on a Bridge"

[From a hundred-poem sequence composed at Kasuga Shrine during the Fourth Month of 1451].

> Where the mountain folk
> have all vanished
> > from the peak
> and its plank bridge,*
> now stars
> > passing through the night
> and fireflies
> > make their way.

♦ ♦ ♦ ♦ ♦

yamabito wa / taenuru mine no / kakehashi ni /
yowataru hoshi to / hotaru to zo yuku

*A rope and plank bridge suspended over a mountain gorge.

28   *"Dream Disturbed by Reeds"*

[From a hundred-poem sequence composed at Kasuga Shrine during the
Fourth Month of 1451].

How cruel
           the voice
that bars me
                from traveling
the way of dreams.
Not a man,
              but still a gate guard
is that wind
              in the reeds.

✦ ✦ ✦ ✦ ✦

kayoiyuku / yumeji tōsanu / koe mo ushi /
hito naranu ogi no / kaze no sekimori

[From a hundred-poem sequence composed at Hasedera during the Fourth Month of 1451].

> Resenting
> > the moon
> on the rim
> > of the mountains,
> my hut has grown old—
> while I
> > waited for it to rise,
> and
> > lamented when it set.

✦ ✦ ✦ ✦ ✦

*yama no ha no / tsuki o uramite / io furinu /
izuru o matsu to / iru o oshimu to*

30   *"Bamboo"*

[From a hundred-poem sequence composed at Hasedera Shrine during the Fourth Month of 1451].

Even for one
                    alone
        the world
                is a place
                        of trials;
        with what
                    feeling, then,
        must the parent bamboos watch
        their young shoots
                        as they grow!

♦ ♦ ♦ ♦ ♦

*hitori dani / yo wa uki mono o / oyatake no /
ko no oitatsu o / aware to ya miru*

"Reminiscing"

[From a fifty-poem sequence composed at Hasedera in 1451].

All these images
from
    a world
        of long ago —
of what good are they?
Pine winds, come—
            please blow away
these unforgotten
        dreams.*

♦ ♦ ♦ ♦ ♦

omokage ni / mishi yo no arite / nani ka sen /
wasurenu yume o / harae matsukaze

*An allusive variation on *Shin kokinshū* 1564, by Minamoto Michiteru: Lost in the weeds, / my sleeves rot beneath harsh tears / become autumn frost— / as storm winds blow away / my unforgotten dreams. (asajifu ya / sode ni kuchinishi / aki no shimo / wasurenu yume o / fuku arashi kana)

32   *"Dream"*

[From a hundred-poem sequence composed at Hie Shrine during the
Third Month of 1459].

> Even in
> >   one's sleep,
> it is
> >   dreams of this world
> > >   one sees,
> and of
> >   no other;
> just as there is
> >   no dawning here
> that brings
> >   true awakening.

♦ ♦ ♦ ♦ ♦

nuru ga uchi mo / kono yo no yume no / hoka narade /
makoto ni samuru / akatsuki mo nashi

From among fifty poems composed extemporaneously at the house of the
Governor of Awa [during the Third Month of 1429].

> So clear
>   is the moon
> that the waterless
>   winter sky
> is locked up tight.
> And sweeping
>   over
>   the ice—
> the withering
>   midnight wind.*

♦ ♦ ♦ ♦ ♦

*tsuki sumeba / fuyu no mizu naki / sora tojite /
kōri o harau / yowa no kogarashi*

*An allusive variation on *Kokinshū* 89 (Spring), by Ki no Tsurayuki: The cherry
blossoms / have scattered on the wind / that leaves in its wake / waves that rise and
crest / in a waterless sky. (sakurabana / chırınuru kaze no / nagori ni wa / mizu naki
sora ni / nami zo tachikeru)

34   *"Blossoms Falling in a Garden at Dawn"*

From among the poems composed at the Bureau of Poetry on the twenti-
eth day [of the Third Month of 1429].

> The moon
> > comes to visit
> a garden
> > of stormy winds
> that scatter
> > blossoms—
> its lodging there
> > as fleeting
> as dew glistening
> > at dawn.

✦ ✦ ✦ ✦ ✦

tsuki zo tou / niwa no arashi ni / chiru hana no /
yadori munashiki / akatsuki no tsuyu

"Prayer to the Gods"

Among three poems composed for the monthly poetry meeting at the house of Director of the Imperial Stables of the Right Mochizumi on the twelfth day [of the First Month of 1430].

> Learn it well,
>   then:
> for of the deeds established
> in the Age
>   of Gods,
> only
>   this Way
>   still remains—
> The Way of
>   Words of Yamato.*

♦ ♦ ♦ ♦ ♦

*manabe tada / kami no yo yori no / kotowaza wa /
kono michi nomi no / yamato koto no ha*

---

* Yamato was the ancient name of Japan.

36   *"Dawn Love"*

From among three poems composed for the monthly poetry meeting
at his cottage on the thirteenth day [of the intercalary Eleventh Month
of 1431].

> Think of it
>   as cruel—
> but still
>   it brings back memories:
> that glaring moon
> that had
>   such a distant look
> at the moment
>   of dawn.*

♦ ♦ ♦ ♦ ♦

*uki mono to / nasu mo katami zo / ariake no /
tsurenaku mieshi / to bakari no tsuki*

---

*An allusive variation on *Kokinshū* 625 (Love), by Mibu no Tadamine: Since that
parting / when I saw that distant look / in the late moon's glare, / nothing seems
more to cruel to me / than the hours before dawn. (ariake no / tsurenaku mieshi /
wakare yori / akatsuki bakari / ukimono wa nashi)

"Love, Related to 'Bow'"

From the poems of a sequence composed at the home of the Governor of Awa.

>   Neither tip
>   nor base
>   of the bow
>   of spindlewood*
>   does my body know—
>   as on love's
>   paths still untried
>   my heart is
>   drawn along.

✦ ✦ ✦ ✦ ✦

ukimi ni wa / azusa no mayumi / moto sue mo /
shiranu koiji ni / hiku kokoro kana

---

*An erotic image suggestive of smooth skin.

38   *"Dream"*

From the poems of a sequence composed at the home of the Governor of Awa.

If one may not think
of what one sees
in one's sleep
as reality
then what use
could there be
in dreams
when one is awake?

♦ ♦ ♦ ♦ ♦

nuru ga uchi ni / miru o utsutsu to / omowazu wa /
samete no yume no / kai ya nakaran

Requested by the Ōhira Oki Lay Monk from Tosa when he came to my
cottage on the eighteenth day [of the Fourth Month of 1432].

> So deep
>   the night!
> Who is there
>   for me to ask—
> about the dream
> I awakened from
>   too soon,
> my taper still
>   far from burned down?

✦ ✦ ✦ ✦ ✦

*yo ya fukashi / tare ni towamashi / tomoshibi no /
nokori ōku mo / samuru yume kana*

40   *"Cuckoo Before the Moon"*

Written for the monthly poetry meeting at the Kai'inji [held by Archbishop Kōkyō] on the 25th day [of the Fifth Month of 1432].

Was that the moon
                calling?
I wonder, following as far
as its
        cloudy path—
to where,
            close by the light,
I hear the voice
            of a cuckoo.

✦ ✦ ✦ ✦ ✦

*kumoji yuku / tsuki no koe ka to / tadoru made /
hikari ni chikaki / hototogisu kana*

From the monthly poetry meeting at my cottage on the third day of the Second Month [of 1443].

> To one
>
>   who wanders
>
> in the gloom
>
>   of this world
>
> even
>
>   a pine torch
>
> held aloft
>
>   by a peasant's hand
>
> is a
>
>   happy sight.

✦ ✦ ✦ ✦ ✦

kuraki yo wa / matsu furitatete / yuku shizu no /
hikari ni au mo / sazo na ureshiki

42   *"Fireflies Flying Over a River"*

From a three-poem set for debate held at the house of the Director of the Imperial Stables of the Right on the third day of the Fifth Month [of 1433], for which I made final judgments.*

> On Taki River
> waves shatter
>   into pieces;
> and
>   from
>   the rocks,
> fire
>   seems to come bursting forth—
> scattering
>   fireflies.

✦ ✦ ✦ ✦ ✦

*takigawa ya / nami mo kudakete / ishi no hi no /
idekeru mono to / chiru hotaru kana*

Shūgihan. A poem contest during which poems composed on set topics were discussed and voted upon. In this case, it appears that final judgment was left to Shōtetsu as the "master."

From the monthly poetry meeting held at my cottage on the 25th day [of
the Sixth Month of 1433].

> Withering all
> in its roar
>   across the fields
> comes an evening storm—
> and above,
>   carried on its winds:
> You clouds!
>   You driven leaves!

✦ ✦ ✦ ✦ ✦

*fukishiori / nowaki o narasu / yūdachi no /
kaze no ue naru / kumo yo konoha yo*

44   *"Love, Related to 'Smoke'"*

From the first monthly poetry meeting at the home of the Senior Assistant of the Central Affairs Ministry, held on the 27th day [of the Eighth Month of 1433].

> How I envy them!
> For it is not smoke
>   rising
> from
>   fires of passion
> that surrounds
>   those villagers
> meeting
>   at break of day.

✦ ✦ ✦ ✦ ✦

urayamashi / omoi yori tatsu / kemuri ni mo /
aranu asake ni / majiru satobito

Written on the tenth day of the Tenth Month [of 1433] when Mochitoyo, Assistant in the Board of Censors, and others came for the first meeting after the new cottage of Sōzei had been completed.

Truly a cottage
where
    the leaves
        on the grasses
have
    blossomed as words—
a place, too,
        blessed abundantly
by the work
      of rain and dew.

✦ ✦ ✦ ✦ ✦

koto no ha no / hana saku kusa no / iori kana /
sazo ametsuyu mo / megumiokiken

46   *"Passing Like a Dream"*

Written [during the Tenth Month of 1433] when I accompanied the Former Governor of Awa and Director of the Imperial Stables of the Right to a temple called Hōshōji.

In
    the space
        of one
            night
I seem to forget
        so much!
How is it,
    then,
that my dreams
        of the past
remain to me
        so clear?

✦ ✦ ✦ ✦ ✦

yo no ma ni mo / wasururu mono o / inishie no /
yume wa sadaka ni / nado nokoruran

From the monthly poetry meeting at the home of the Assistant in the Board of Censors on the sixteenth day [of the Eleventh Month of 1435].

> In shadows
> > deep
> stand pines
> > that through
> > > countless ages
> dropped needles
> > numberless,
> leaving a courtyard
> > thick with dust
> I pray
> > the wind
> > > not to sweep away.

✦ ✦ ✦ ✦ ✦

*kage fukaki / matsu no furu ha ni / chiyo no kazu /
tsumoreru niwa no / chiri na harai so*

48   *"First Love in Old Age"*

Written for the monthly poetry meeting at his cottage on the twelfth day
of the Twelfth Month [of 1435].

It started to burn,
but the firewood
                    of my passion
has rotted through.
Now I wait
                    in the dying dusk
for the smoke
                    to fade away.

♦ ♦ ♦ ♦ ♦

*takisomuru / omoi no takigi / kuchihatete /
kiemu yūbe no / keburi o zo matsu*

49   *"Buddhism"*

Written at a residence in Yokawa on the fifteenth day [of the Fourth Month of 1442, while on a circuit of the Three Compounds on Mount Hiei].

Out of
            the stillness
of my own breast
                        emerges
the rising moon;
and when I turn to look at it—
the moon
            in clumps of cloud.

♦ ♦ ♦ ♦ ♦

shizuka naru / waga mune wakete / izuru tsuki /
furisakemireba / murakumo no tsuki

50   *"Reminiscing"*

From the monthly poetry meeting of the Isshiki Master of the Left Capital [on the 23d day of the First Month of 1447].

> No one
> 　　　　remains now
> for me to spend my time with—
> I who
> 　　　　in the past
> was known to spurn
> 　　　　　　　the company
> of those who had grown old.

✦ ✦ ✦ ✦ ✦

majirowamu / hito koso nakere / oinuru o /
mukashi itoishi / kokoro narai ni

Presented after receiving a topic from Lord Ichijō for a poem to be included in a hundred-poem votive sequence [during the Third Month of 1447].

> First comes
>   a sound;
> then before
>   the showers begin
> the pattern
>   of clouds
> and birds* is torn
>   in tatters
> among trees
>   blown by mountain winds.

♦ ♦ ♦ ♦ ♦

oto wa shite / furikonu saki ni / yūdachi no /
kumotori sawagu / kigi no yamakaze

**Kumotori,* here referring to both actual clouds and birds and to a decorative pattern involving images of the same used to adorn court robes.

52   *"One Call from a Cuckoo"*

From the monthly poetry meeting at my cottage [on the twentieth day of the Fourth Month of 1447].

As if to say—
"Isn't it true
                for men, as well:
that the more the words,
the less
        they are of value?"—
the cuckoo does not call again.

♦ ♦ ♦ ♦ ♦

hototogisu / hito mo kotoba no / ōkaru wa /
shina sukunashi to / mata ya koe senu

"Summer Writing Brush"

From the monthly poetry meeting of the Master of the Left Capital on the 23d day of the Fifth Month [of 1447].

> When I
>   look upon
> the rich sheen
>   of summer hairs
> in my new brush,*
> I am saddened
>   by a deer
> drawn
>   at night
>   to a hunter's torch.

✦ ✦ ✦ ✦ ✦

*atarashiki / natsuke irokoki / fude o mite /
tomoshi no shika no / yoru zo kanashiki*

*A writing brush made of deer hair.

54 *"Not Knowing Whether Love Has Come to an End"*

From the monthly poetry meeting at the home of the Director of the Imperial Stables of the Right on the 24th day [of the Eighth Month of 1447].

The one
                who promised
now has gone off
                        who knows where,
a bird flying off
at morning,
                into the sky,
leaving me
                in evening's wake.

+ + + + +

chigiritsuru / hito no yukue wa / sora tobishi /
asa no tori no / yūgure no ato

From the monthly poetry meeting at the home of the Director of the Imperial Stables of the Right on the 24th day [of the Eighth Month of 1447].

> And what
>   more than this
> should I ever have to lament:
> that
>   I must live
>   now,
> when I can meet no Buddha—
> not of the past,
>   or yet to come.

✦ ✦ ✦ ✦ ✦

nanigoto o / sara ni nagekamu / nochi saki no /
hotoke ni awanu / yo ni sumu mi wa

56   *"The Remaining Moon"*

When the Bizen Lay Monk Jōgan held his first monthly poetry meeting on the 27th day [of the Eighth Month of 1447].

In the moon
                    at dawn
I see
        one example
                    at last—
of how
            even
in this world,
                    there are times
when grieving
                can make things stay.

♦ ♦ ♦ ♦ ♦

akuru ma no / tsuki ni zo mitsuru / kono yo ni mo /
oshimeba nokoru / narai ari to wa

"Wisteria at a Famous Place"

At Takasago,
the glow
            from pines on the peak
is wisteria,
there where evening
                        is suspended
from the voice
            of the bell.*

♦ ♦ ♦ ♦ ♦

takasago no / onoe ni niou / matsu no fuji /
yūbe zo kane no / koe ni kakareru

*The vespers bell that calls the temple community to prayer.

58   *"A Warbler Announcing Spring at Morning"*

How does he
                    know
that spring
                    has come to the world?
From
          within
                    the cage
where he wakes
                    from sleep
                                        at daybreak—
the sound
          of a warbler's call.

✦ ✦ ✦ ✦ ✦

yo wa haru to / ikade shiruramu / ko no uchi ni /
nete no asake no / uguisu no koe

"An Animal, in Spring"

The gloom of dusk.
An ox
          from out
                    in the fields
comes walking my way;
and along
          the hazy road
I encounter
          no one.

✦ ✦ ✦ ✦ ✦

*yūmagure / nogai no ushi wa / ayumikite /
kasumeru michi ni / au hito mo nashi*

60   *"Animal, Related to 'Blossoms' "*

Even from
            blossoms
I learn
        what it is
                that I am:
no more than a beast,
devoid of
            proper feeling,
howling away
                at the clouds.

✦ ✦ ✦ ✦ ✦

hana nite mo / mi wa kokoro naki / kedamono no /
kumo ni hoeken / tameshi o zo shiru

"Lark in the Clouds"

A calling
            lark
stays aloft
            up in the sky,
while its field
is turned
            under
                by the plow—
leaving no bed
            in the grass below.

✦ ✦ ✦ ✦ ✦

naku hibari / sora ni aru ma ni / sukikaesu /
tazura no kusa mo / toko wa naku shite

62   *"Falling Blossoms"*

Blossoms opened,

           then fell

in the space

        of just

           one night,

as if

      in a dream—

no more

        to be mistaken

for white clouds

          on the peak.*

✦ ✦ ✦ ✦ ✦

*sakeba chiru / yo no ma no hana no / yume no uchi ni /
yagate magirenu / mine no shirakumo*

---

*An allusion to a scene in the "Lavender" chapter of *The Tale of Genji* in which a disappointed Genji wishes he could disappear and his existence be mistaken for a dream.

Here
        in my bedchamber
my folding fan,
                shining white,
is set aglow—
by the heat
            of my passion,
alight
        with swarming
                    fireflies.

✦ ✦ ✦ ✦ ✦

neya no uchi no / shiroki ōgi ya / kogasuran /
sudaku hotaru no / moyuru omoi ni

64　*"Short Summer Night"*

While I swatted
at
　　the sound of
　　　　　　mosquitoes
getting through
　　　　　　the cloth
of my thin summer robes—
suddenly
　　　　the day had dawned.

＋ ＋ ＋ ＋ ＋

*natsugoromo / tamoto ni tōru / ka no koe o /
uchiharau ma ni / akuru yowa kana*

"Summer Moon"

How cool
            is the breeze
that moves
                the trees
                    up high
on the mountain ridge—
as the fan
            of the rising moon
is raised
            into the night.

✦ ✦ ✦ ✦ ✦

yama no ha no / ki o ugokaseru / kaze suzushi /
ōgi o agete / izuru tsukiyo ni

66   *"Fireflies"*

So bereft
   was she,
lost in grief for her lost child—
that her
   dead spirit
may now be
    one of those fireflies,
in night's gloom,
    burning on.*

✦ ✦ ✦ ✦ ✦

*sanomi ko o / omoishi hito no / naki tama ya /
hotaru to narite / yami ni moyuran*

*An allusion to *Goshūishū* 1162 (Miscellaneous), by Izumi Shikibu: So forlorn am I
/ that when I see a firefly / out on the marshes, / it looks like my soul rising / from
my body in longing. (mono omoeba / sawa no hotaru o / waga mi yori /
akugareizuru / tama ka to zo miru). The original poem expresses grief after losing
a lover, but Shōtetsu's poem has in mind the death of her daughter, Koshikibu no
Naishi, which left Izumi Shikibu wandering in the "gloom" of her heart—a
conventional metaphor for the love of a parent for a child.

This is coolness—
the wind
                burnishing the sky
as it
        blows clouds
that break
                like waves
                        scattering
'round the white jewel
                    of the moon.

♦ ♦ ♦ ♦ ♦

suzushisa wa / sora o migakite / fuku kaze ni /
kumo no nami chiru / tsuki no shiratama

68   *"By a Spring at Dusk"*

This day
            that I spent
by a spring
                till it got dark,
never tiring—
I must not forget it later,
sitting by
            a small coal fire.

♦ ♦ ♦ ♦ ♦

kururu made / akazu izumi ni / mukau hi wa /
omoiwasurenu / uzumibi no moto

Ah, the feel
                on my skin
of a summer robe,
                    still damp
in the morning!
Wait, then,
            don't dry it
                        yet—
you wind blowing
            low in the trees!

✦ ✦ ✦ ✦ ✦

natsugoromo / mi ni tsuku hodo no / asajimeri /
hosu na yo shibashi / kigi no shitakaze

70   *"Early Autumn"*

A single leaf
                  falls,
a single flower
                  blossoms,
both
      proclaiming spring,
and
      announcing autumn—
now that autumn
                  has arrived.

♦ ♦ ♦ ♦ ♦

hitoha chiru / hitohana sakite / haru o tsuge /
aki o shiraseshi / aki wa kinikeri

If only
　　　they knew
that tonight
　　　　the clouds make a path
for the stars
　　　to meet—
then dogs
　　　would not bark at them,
no matter
　　　how late the hour.*

♦ ♦ ♦ ♦ ♦

hoshiai no / michi to shi shiraba / kedamono no /
kumo ni wa hoeji / sayo fukenu to mo

*Ancient Chinese legend had it that the Herdboy (Altair) and the Weaver Maiden
(Vega)—lovers kept apart by the King of Heaven—were allowed to meet once a year,
on the night of the seventh day of the seventh month, known as *Tanabata*.

72   *"Miscanthus* in Early Autumn"*

Beneath
          a boulder—
miscanthus in disarray.
It seems
          not to know
some things
               will not be moved,
this first wind
               of autumn.

♦ ♦ ♦ ♦ ♦

fukimidasu / iwamoto susuki / ugokinaki /
tokoro mo shiranu / aki no hatsukaze

*A plant resembling pampas grass, with long stalks topped with white plumes each autumn.

As my heart ascends
into
    the clear,
        I gaze upon
the clearing
        moon within—
forgetting
        the other moon
midway through
        an autumn night.

✦ ✦ ✦ ✦ ✦

suminoboru / kokoro ni sumeru / tsuki o mite /
tsuki o wasururu / aki no sayonaka

74   *"Autumn Coming to a Remote Hut"*

Even the mountain wind
seems
            nothing like
                        yesterday's.
And here
            I had thought
not even autumn
                        would know
of my house
            hidden in the trees.

✦ ✦ ✦ ✦ ✦

yamakaze mo / kinō ni zo ninu / aki ni dani /
shirareji to omou / kogakure no yado

Worse
        than
                the heartache
of the blossoms
                in spring—
the moon
           going down,
with the autumn wind
                  failing
to scatter abroad
           its light.

✦ ✦ ✦ ✦ ✦

haru no hana / uki ni zo masaru / iru tsuki no /
hikari chirasade / okuru akikaze

76   *"Mist"*

Is the hour so late?
In the moonlight,
                    the sound
of the storm
                has ceased;
in the mist,
            all is quiet now,
at midnight
            below the mountain.

✦ ✦ ✦ ✦ ✦

fukenuru ka / tsuki ni arashi no / koe taete /
kiri ni shizumaru / yowa no yamamoto

"Winter Paddies"

Mountain paddies—
where after
       the harvests
the rice stocks decay:
tufts of snow
       lined up in rows
above
    the water's sheen.

♦ ♦ ♦ ♦ ♦

*oyamada ya / karishi inakuki / kuchinagara /
yuki o naraburu / mizu no ue kana*

78   *"Winter Birds"*

How is one
                to sleep?
On a frosty night
                        in winter
the sky
        is clear;
passing through
                    the storm winds—
calls from
            a flock of birds.

✦ ✦ ✦ ✦ ✦

ikaga nemu / fuyu no shimoyo no / sora saete /
arashi ni wataru / muratori no koe

Still hanging back,
the clouds, too,
                    this evening
seem to hesitate
before
          the untrodden snow
of the plank bridge*
                    on the peak.

✦ ✦ ✦ ✦ ✦

*watarikane / kumo mo yūbe o / nao tadoru /
ato naki yuki no / mine no kakehashi*

*Kakehashi, a rope and plank bridge spanning a mountain gorge.

80   *"Hail in the Brushwood"*

What looked
                like rice
left behind
                by foresters
taking a break
from gathering
                    brushwood—
turned out instead
                    to be hail.

✦ ✦ ✦ ✦ ✦

yamagatsu no / shii no karishiba / karemeshi no /
nokoru to miru wa / arare narikeri

"Fishing Weirs"*

How carefree they are—
the spirits
        of those
                fish
frolicking
        in leaves
borne along by river waves,
not far
        from wooden weirs.

♦ ♦ ♦ ♦ ♦

*hakanashi ya / ajiro ni chikaki / kawanami no /
ko no ha ni asobu / hio no kokoro wa*

**Ajiro,* wooden stakes placed in a river to catch fish on their way downstream.

82   *"Frost on Cold Grass"*

In the withered
                    grass
of a flower garden
                        of frost
in a winter field,
even now butterflies play—
flakes of
            swirling snow.

✦ ✦ ✦ ✦ ✦

kusa karuru / fuyuno no shimo no / hanazono ni /
ima mo kochō no / asobu yuki kana

"Moss Path Buried by Snow"

Trodding on
           moss,
trodding on
           tufts of grass,
I trample
        about
where not a footprint
              marks the way
of a mountain
        path
          in the snow.

✦ ✦ ✦ ✦ ✦

koke o fumi / odoro o fumite / ato mo naki /
yuki ni yamaji no / atari o zo yuku

84   *"Hail Again at Dawn"*

At break of day,
on the leaves
                of my garden court—
jewels of hail:
just one,
            and then another
falling,
            in forlorn silence.

✦ ✦ ✦ ✦ ✦

ariake no / niwa no konoha ni / tamaarare /
hitotsu futatsu / ochite sabishiki

"Parting"

Not
      a single hue,
  not a tree
        or blade of grass
but reminds me
          of you—
when we part
         and I steal off
on a path
       faint with dawn light.*

✦ ✦ ✦ ✦ ✦

kusa mo ki mo / omokage naranu / iro zo naki /
uki kinuginu no / shinonome no michi

---

*An allusive variation on *Fūgashū* 1214 (Love), by Emperor Fushimi: In the midst of love / I see one thing in everything / within my gaze: / not a tree, not a blade of grass / but is a vision of you. (koishisa ni / naritatsu naka no / nagame ni wa / omokage naranu / kusa mo ki mo nashi.

86   *"Love in Spring"*

In evening's gloom,
I thought
     I saw
          the dim form
of the one I love,
there now
       as a memento
in the haze
        'round the dawn moon.

✦ ✦ ✦ ✦ ✦

yūmagure / sore ka to mieshi / omokage mo /
kasumu zo katami / ariake no tsuki

To her house
                    I come,
in vain, it seems,
                    and turn to go,
when I hear
                    a sound
that makes
                    me, too, fall silent,
just standing there,
                    wondering.

♦ ♦ ♦ ♦ ♦

yado toeba / yagate yametsuru / mono no ne ni /
ware mo oto sede / tachi zo yasurau

88   *"Love, Related to 'the Moon' "*

Unforgettable
is the image
                    that from my eyes
descends in tears—
showering onto
                    my sleeves
with moonlight
                    at break of day.

✦ ✦ ✦ ✦ ✦

wasurarenu / namida no uchi no / omokage mo /
sode ni koboruru / ariake no tsuki

If for
        even
                one night
the grasses
                of my passion
were cut and gathered,
ah, what
            a pile
                    they would make—
a mountain reaching
                    the clouds.

✦ ✦ ✦ ✦ ✦

yo no ma ni mo / waga koigusa o / karitsumite /
yama to shi nasaba / kumo ya kakaramu

90   *"Birds Lodging in Evening Groves"*

Below the mountain,
in the rain
            of evening,
doves are calling—
all in a row
            on branches
darkened by engulfing clouds.

♦ ♦ ♦ ♦ ♦

yamamoto no / yūbe no ame ni / naku hato no /
narabu kozue zo / kumogakureyuku

"Pines by the Eaves"

Ah, loneliness:
I need only abandon it
to
    the pine wind
from the mountains
                by my eaves,
and it seems
        not to blow at all.

✦ ✦ ✦ ✦ ✦

*sabishisa o / nokiba no yama no / matsukaze ni /
makasehatsureba / fuku to shi mo nashi*

92   *"Travel"*

The gloom of dusk.
A boat here
        all tethered up,
with no one
        around.
It will be
        along this riverbank
that I rest
        from travel tonight.

✦ ✦ ✦ ✦ ✦

yūmagure / fune wa tsunagite / hito mo nashi /
kono kawara ni ya / tabimakura sen

"Travel"

There it
        remains,
as if to recall memories
of that midnight
           dream
that parted
        from the mountain peak
where now
        a cloud trails away.

✦ ✦ ✦ ✦ ✦

kaerimiru / katami zo nokoru / yowa no yume /
wakareshi mine ni / kakaru yokogumo

94   *"Travel"*

Horses whinny,
cocks crow,
                    as travelers
rise and go away—
the village
                    overflowing
with the sound
                    of their voices.

✦ ✦ ✦ ✦ ✦

*uma ibui / niwatori nakite / tabibito no /
idetatsu koe zo / sato ni amareru*

"Boat on an Inlet"

The world
           of men:
among grasses
                floating free
in an inlet,
an untethered boat
                    tossed about
by waves
          that bring it
                      to shore.*

♦ ♦ ♦ ♦ ♦

*hito no yo wa / ne o hanaretaru / kusa ga e ni /
tsunaganu fune no / kishi ni yoru nami*

---

* A vague allusion to *Kokinshū* 1030 (Miscellaneous), by Ono no Komachi: In my
forlorn state / I feel like a floating reed / ready to break free / at the roots and drift
away— / if there were waters to tempt me. (wabinureba / mi o ukikusa no / ne o
taete / sasou mizu araba / inamu to zo omou) and perhaps also to *Man'yōshū* 354,
by Sami Mansei: Our life in this world: / to what shall I compare it? / It is like a boat
/ rowing out at break of day, / leaving not a trace behind. (yo no naka o / nani ni
tatoemu / asabiraki / kogiinishi fune no / ato naki ga goto)

96   *"Bridge in the Rain"*

From
        the river's edge,
stretching
            off
                to the mountain ridge,
stands a rainbow—
a bridge
        that makes no sound
when crossed
            by passing rain.

♦ ♦ ♦ ♦ ♦

*kawabe yori / yama no ha kakete / tatsu niji no /
oto senu hashi o / wataru ame kana*

Make haste,

        people!

No matter

        which of the Ways

you choose

        to learn,

in old age

        your heart

            gives out,

making

        every effort vain.

✦ ✦ ✦ ✦ ✦

isoge hito / izure no michi o / manabu to mo /
oi wa kokoro no / tsukite kai nashi

98   *"Reminiscing"*

So far
        to go yet
on the long Way of Poetry—
when the daylight
                ends.
How I wish
            I had
                the body
I had
        back when I began!

✦ ✦ ✦ ✦ ✦

*shikishima no / michi tōku shite / hi wa kurenu /
koshikata hodo no / waga mi to mogana*

"Rain at the Window"

In the dark
              of night
my heart
              sinks
                      into the rain
striking
          the window—
then floating back up
                      with things
that happened
              long, long ago.

♦ ♦ ♦ ♦ ♦

*kuraki yo no / mado utsu ame ni / waga kokoro /
shizumeba ukabu / yoyo no furugoto*

100   *"Monkey"*

Such a world
                is ours—
where all must
                submit themselves
to courtyard teachings,*
even a monkey
                bound to learn
from the one who holds his chain.

✦ ✦ ✦ ✦ ✦

*tsunagaruru / tegai no saru no / manabi dani /
niwa no oshie wa / aru yo narazu ya*

Niwa no oshie, the teachings of one's parents, so called in reference to a scene in the
life of Confucius when he stops his son in the courtyard to instruct him.

"Buddhism, Related to 'Blossoms'"

With every
　　　　　new spring
the blossoms
　　　　　　speak not a word,
yet expound
　　　　　the law—
knowing
　　　　　what is at its heart
from the scattering
　　　　　　storm winds.

✦ ✦ ✦ ✦ ✦

*haru goto ni / hana mono iwade / toku nori no /
kokoro shirarete / chiru arashi kana*

102   *"Visitors Are Rare at a Mountain Home"*

A reply
        will come
as an echo
            in the mountains,
so it would seem;
but if one says
                nothing first,
there will be
            no answer
                    to hear.

♦ ♦ ♦ ♦ ♦

kotau beki / sazo yamabiko mo / aruramedo /
mono iwazareba / kiku koto mo nashi

"House in the Fields"

By a field-hut,
a longbow
           is left standing—
with no one
           about.
No doubt he'll
           be coming back
to watch
           over the fields
                      tonight.*

✦ ✦ ✦ ✦ ✦

kariio ni / yumi tateokite / hito mo nashi /
yamada moru o ya / yoru kaerikomu

---

*A paddy guard employed to keep deer and other animals from destroying crops.

104 *"Feelings Distant Before the Moon"*

Closing
   my eyes,
I need only
    to ponder
and I see it all—
the moon shining
     brightly
over Yamato
    and Cathay.*

✦ ✦ ✦ ✦ ✦

me o tojite / omoeba itodo / mukaimiru /
tsuki zo sayakeki / yamato morokoshi

Morokoshi, a name for China.

Written for a poem sequence at a certain place on the sixteenth day [of the
First Month of 1449].

> The mountains—
>   not hazy
> yet, with the snow too
>   unable
> to begin falling;
> above the winds
>   of a storm—
> racks of cloud,
>   frozen.

+ + + + +

*yama wa mada / kasumanu yuki mo / furikanete /
arashi no ue ni / kōru kumo kana*

106   *"Bell at an Old Temple"*

From a poem sequence composed when Fujiwara Toshinaga and more than ten others came to my cottage on the 26th day [of the First Month of 1449].

> Close by
>   the eaves,
> where amidst
>   *shinobu* ferns*
> the pines
>   grow old—
> moss
>   has covered
>   the bell,
> muffling the sound
>   of its voice.

✦ ✦ ✦ ✦ ✦

nokiba naru / shinobu ni majiru / matsu furite /
kane ni koke musu / koe mumoru nari

---

*Shinobu[gusa], a fern whose name is a partial homophone with the verb *shinobu*, "to think fondly of the past."

"Loving in Secret"

Written for a poem sequence at the home of the Tō Lay-Monk of
Shimōsa, Sokin, on the fourth day of the Second Month [of 1449].

> Ah, if only
> > the sight
> of blossoms
> > at close of day
> would
> > stay with me!
> Then though asleep,
> > > I would not part
> from
> > my dream
> > > of a spring night.

♦ ♦ ♦ ♦ ♦

kururu ma no / hana no omokage / mi ni sowaba /
nete mo wakareji / haru no yo no yume

I08   *"Cedars in Front of a Shrine"*

From among poems composed for a poem sequence composed when I visited the quarters of Nihō Shōnin of the Myōkōji on the sixth day [of the Second Month of 1449].

> Surely
> 　　　a sign
> that the world
> 　　　　　is in order,
> the nation subdued—
> by the shrine
> 　　　　of the gods,
> halberd cedars*
> 　　　　standing tall.

✦ ✦ ✦ ✦ ✦

yo o osame / kuni o shizumuru / shirushi mo ya / kami no yashiro ni / hokosugi tatsuran

*Hokosugi, a variety of cryptomeria, a cedarlike evergreen with long straight trunks with branches only toward the top.

"Bell in Faint Dusk"

From a poem sequence composed when I visited the quarters of the Miidera monk Chōsan at Butsuchi'in on the seventh day [of the Second Month of 1449].

As darkness
                comes on
still I will think
                fondly of it—
the dream
          of the night
from which
          the sound of this bell
awakened me
          at break of day.

✦ ✦ ✦ ✦ ✦

kururu ma mo / mata zo koishiki / kono kane no /
akatsuki no koe ni / sameshi yo no yume

110   *"River"*

From the monthly poetry meeting at the quarters of Chōsan on the tenth day [of the Second Month of 1449].

How can
        the number
of people
        in this world
                change?
As the river
        flows,
the water
        is never
the same,
        nor does it end.*

✦ ✦ ✦ ✦ ✦

*yo no hito no / kazu ya wa kawaru / yuku kawa mo /
moto no mizu ni wa / arade taeseji*

---

*An allusion to the first sentence of Kamo no Chōmei's famous *Hōjōki* ("The Ten-Foot Square Hut"): "On and on flows the river, but the water is never the same."

"Azaleas"

From a poem sequence composed when I first visited the Isshiki Master
of the Left Capital Norichika after the construction of the latter's Meeting
Hall and garden on the second day [of the Third Month 1449].

> On
>   the roadside,
> beneath a crag—
>   azaleas.
> Who can it have been,
> to take off
>   her crimson skirt,
> leave it here,
>   and go away?

✦ ✦ ✦ ✦ ✦

*michinobe no / iwamoto tsutsuji / kurenai no /
akamo nugisute / tare ka inikemu*

112   *"Seeing a Few Blossoms Fall"*

From the monthly poetry meeting at the quarters of Chōsan on the sixteenth day [of the Third Month of 1449].

> Blossoms, indeed,
>   are these:
> from leaves of green
>   trails the net
> of a spider's web,
> where
>   from a thread dangles
> a single tuft
>   of snow.

✦ ✦ ✦ ✦ ✦

hana ya kore / aoba ni sugaku / sasagani no /
ito ni kakareru / yuki no hitomura

"Love, Related to 'Spring Appearing'"

From the monthly poetry meeting at the quarters of the Butsuchi'in Bishop Chōsan on the sixteenth [of the Third Month of 1449].

> I try to hide it,
> but still my love
> > > burns within—
> grasses of springtime
> > > > whose colors
> show the more
> > > clearly
> for a layer
> > > of snow.

✦ ✦ ✦ ✦ ✦

uzumedomo / shitamoe masaru / omoigusa /
yukima sadaka ni / iro ya miyuran

114   *"Reminiscing"*   ✓

From among the poems of a hundred-poem sequence sponsored by a certain person as a votive offering to the myriad gods on the eighth day [of the Fourth Month of 1449].

> From
> > long ago
> I have been
> > coming along,
> never arriving.
> Even the old
> > have far to go:
> for that is the way
> > with this Way.

♦ ♦ ♦ ♦ ♦

*mukashi yori / kite mo sakai ni / irazariki /
oite mo tōki / michi wa kono michi*

"Night Rain"

From among the poems of a hundred-poem sequence sponsored by a certain person as a votive offering to the myriad gods on the eleventh day [of the Fourth Month of 1449].

> In
>   the falling rain
> at the bottom
>   of my heart
> are my friends—
>   all there
> but only
>   as images
> dark in the gloom
>   of the past.

✦ ✦ ✦ ✦ ✦

*furu ame no / soko no kokoro ni / tomo wa mina /
aru mo mukashi no / kuraki omokage*

116   *"Evening Bell"*

From a poem sequence composed as a votive offering by a certain person, at a place called Eisen'an, on the eighth day [of the Fifth Month of 1449].

> Falling
> 　　　　on the robes
> of those
> 　　　　who live in the clear,*
> they deepen
> 　　　　　　a color
> already black as ink—
> those bells
> 　　　　　ringing in the dusk.

✦ ✦ ✦ ✦ ✦

sumu hito no / koromo ni ochite / sumizome no /
iro o fukamuru / yūgure no kane

Sumu hito, a double entendre referring to clerics wearing dark robes who live (*sumu*) "in the clear" (*sumu*) light of Buddhist truth.

From the monthly poetry meeting at the home of the Master of the Palace Table Office held on the eighteenth day [of the Seventh Month of 1449].

> Ah, solitude—
> no fragrance
>   from the blossoms,
> no birds
>   about;
> in moss,
>   an aging orchard
> and
>   the autumn wind.*

✦ ✦ ✦ ✦ ✦

sabishisa wa / hana mo niowazu / tori mo izu /
koke ni furitaru / sono no akikaze

---

*An allusion to *Shin kokinshū* 361, by Monk Jakuren (1139?–1202): Ah, solitude— / it is not the sort of thing / that has a color. / Mountains lined with black pine / on an evening in autumn. (sabishisa wa / sono iro to shi mo / nakarikeri / maki tatsu yama no / aki no yūgure)

118   *"Bells at Evening on a Mountain"*

From a poem sequence at the home of the Master of Palace Repairs on the nineteenth day [of the Seventh Month of 1449].

> What a noise
>   they make!
> In the groves
>   up on the peak
> in the gloom of dusk,
> the bells toll,
>   and chiming in—
> the birds, too,
>   and the storm winds.

✦ ✦ ✦ ✦ ✦

*sawagu nari / mine no hayashi no / yūmagure /
tsukiidasu kane ni / tori mo arashi mo*

"Lamp, in Seclusion"

From a poem sequence at the home of the Bizen Lay Monk Jōgan on the eithth day [of the Tenth Month of 1449].

> The image I saw
> remains there
> > in the lamplight.
> Waking
> > from a dream,
> I see
> > something
> > > looking like
> the spirit
> > of one grown old.

✦ ✦ ✦ ✦ ✦

omokage no / nokoru tomoshibi / yume samete /
furinishi hito no / tama ka to zo miru

120   *"Boat on an Inlet"*

From the monthly poetry meeting at the home of the Senior Assistant in the Punishments Ministry on the ninth day [of the Tenth Month of 1449].

Owner
          unknown:
at evening,
               by an inlet,
with no one
               around—
just
     a raincloak
               and a pole
left alone there
               in a skiff.

♦ ♦ ♦ ♦ ♦

nushi shiranu / irie no yūbe / hito nakute /
mino to sao to no / fune ni nokoreru

"Remaining Geese"

From the monthly poetry meeting at the home of the Master of the Left
Capital on the 23d day [of the Tenth Month of 1449].

> In a sky
> > filled
> with frost
> > on a chilly night,
> a goose calls,
> > falling
> into
> > paddies,
> > > where cedars
> stand
> > in dawn moonlight.

✦ ✦ ✦ ✦ ✦

sora ni mitsu / shimoyo no kari mo / nakiochite /
tanaka no sugi yo / ariake no tsuki

122   *"Old Love, in Winter"*

From a poem sequence at the home of the Bizen Lay Monk Jōgan on the 23d day [of the Eleventh Month of 1449].

> Ah, let me forget!
> For now my thoughts are as thick
> as once
>   was my hair—
> black then, but
>   now frosty
> as Isonokami's sands.

♦ ♦ ♦ ♦ ♦

wasurenamu / shimo furu iso no / kamisuji mo /
kurokarishi yo zo / omoimidareshi

"Snow in a Garden"

From the monthly poetry meeting at Ontoku'in on the twentieth day [of the Twelfth Month of 1449].

> Every shrub,
>
>   every tree,
> if one has not forgotten
> where each
>
>   was planted,
> retains beneath
>
>   all covering snow
> a vestige
>
>   of its form.

♦ ♦ ♦ ♦ ♦

kusa mo ki mo / ueshi tokoro o / wasureneba
ato naki yuki ni / nokoru omokage

124   *"Fisherman Visiting an Island"*

From a poem sequence at Myōkōji on the fifteenth day [of the Third Month of 1450].

> Here
>   I am,
>   then,
> away from
>   the cruel world
> on an
>   island—
> trusting
>   the string
>   of my life
> to a line
>   without a hook!

✦ ✦ ✦ ✦ ✦

ukiyo o ba / hanarekojima ni / mi wa aredo /
hari naki tsuri ni / kakeshi tama no o

From the monthly poetry meeting at Ontoku'in on the 27th day [of the Fourth Month of 1450].

> With what harshness
> they come blowing
>   toward me—
> the mountain winds
> from deep
>   within
>   the heart
> of one who asks
>   no lodging.

♦ ♦ ♦ ♦ ♦

hageshiku mo / fukimukau kana / yado towanu /
hito no kokoro no / oku no yamakaze

126   *"Thunder Storm at Sea"*

From the monthly poetry meeting at Jōrakuji on the eighteenth day of
the Fifth Month [of 1450].

Just like the spray
of a whale
                rising for air
in
    the salt breeze—
in the offing,
                one clump of clouds
dropping
            an evening shower.

♦ ♦ ♦ ♦ ♦

ushio fuku / kujira no iki to / mienu beshi /
oki ni hitomura / kudaru yūdachi

From among the poems requested by the Tsukinowa Consultant-Lay Monk Seishō on the 25th day [of the Fifth Month of 1450].

> What is yet
> > to come,
> the past,
> > and the present, too—
> all are
> > no more
> than the light
> > of a lightning flash.
> Such is life
> > in this world!

♦ ♦ ♦ ♦ ♦

*yukusue mo / mukashi mo ima mo / inazuma no /
hikari ni suginu / aware yo no naka*

128   *"Dawn"*

From among poems from a sequence composed at a certain place on the
23d day [of the Sixth Month of 1450].

> The moon—
>   clouded over;
> homes
>   for a thousand leagues—still,
> making not
>   a sound;
> at the edge
>   of a new day,
> the people, too,
>   still dozing.

♦ ♦ ♦ ♦ ♦

*tsuki kumori / chisato shizuka ni / oto mo sezu /
akuru sakai ya / hito mo madoromu*

"Traveler Waiting for Someone"

From a poem sequence at the home of the Master of the Left Capital on the nineteenth day [of the Tenth Month of 1450].

> On the roadside,
> in the light
>   shining all around,
> he looks upward—
> a traveler
>   standing there,
> while somewhere
>   waits a friend.

✦ ✦ ✦ ✦ ✦

michinobe ya / meguru hikage o / augimite /
tateru tabibito / tomo ga matsuran

130   *"Traveler's Inn"*

From among the poems of a fifty-poem sequence composed on the 22d day [of the Second Month of 1451] for the Buddhist services on the first anniversary of the death of a man named Shinkū, a disciple of Master of Discipline Shinkei of the Jūjūshin'in, located in the area around Kiyomizu:

> Ah, the world
> of men:
> at morning,
> someone is born
> while
> at evening
> another life
> is at stake—
> as at Mushiake Straits.

♦ ♦ ♦ ♦ ♦

hito no yo wa / ashita mumare / yūgure ni /
inochi kaketaru / mushiake no seto

"Buddhism, Related to 'Water'"

From among the poems of a seventy-poem sequence at the home of the Master of Palace Repairs on the seventh day [of the Seventh Month of 1451].

> How naturally
> they meet
> > each other in time:
> water
> > not thinking,
> "Come now,
> > take your lodging here!"
> the moon
> > not asking for an inn.

✦ ✦ ✦ ✦ ✦

onozukara / aeru toki kana / yadore to wa /
mizu mo omowazu / tsuki mo tazunezu

132   *"Dawn Mountains"*   ✓

From a poem sequence at the home of the Master of Palace Repairs on the 23d day [of the Seventh Month of 1451].

> Blow then,
>   you storm winds!
> —as in the first
>   light of dawn
> the stars shine
>   brightly,
> in the clear
>   above a peak
> and its
>   one and only pine.

♦ ♦ ♦ ♦ ♦

fuke arashi / akatsuki izuru / hoshi kiyoku /
haretaru mine no / matsu no hitomoto

"Lightning on a Clear Night"

From a poem sequence at the home of the Master of Palace Repairs on the fifth day [of the Eighth Month of 1451].

> Even in its glow
> my heart
>   remains as ever—
> still
>   in the gloom;
> it's for
>   someone
>   other than me—
> this lightning
>   in the night.

✦ ✦ ✦ ✦ ✦

*terashite mo / kokoro wa yami no / mama nareba /
waga mi no yoso ni / sayo no inazuma*

134   *"The Moon Already Gone Down"*

From a poem sequence composed when people came to his cottage [on the fifteenth day of the Eighth Month of 1451].

A thousand leagues
                away,
they will
        be waiting for it—
people in autumn
on the far side
                of the mountain,
where the moon
                just went down.

+ + + + +

chisato made / machi ya izuramu / tsuki irishi /
yama no anata no / aki no morobito

At the home of the Senior Assistant in the Punishments Ministry on the 27th day [of the Ninth Month of 1451].

A rowed-in boat,
run
    aground
        on a sandspit,
oarless
    and alone—
like me,
    weakened
        by the blows
of the buffeting
    bay winds.

♦ ♦ ♦ ♦ ♦

*kogareteshi / fune mo su ni iru / kaji o tae /
mi o urakaze mo / fuki zo yowareru*

136   *"Box Fire"*

From the monthly poetry meeting at the home of the Master of Palace Repairs on the 24th day [of the Tenth Month of 1451].

> Into my box fire*
> I mix
>   fresh chunks of coal;
> then
>   in the light
> of my tranquil
>   chamber
> I wait
>   for
>   the day to dawn.

♦ ♦ ♦ ♦ ♦

*uzumibi ni / sumi sashisoete / shizuka naru /
neya no hikari ni / akuru o zo matsu*

---

* *Uzumibi,* a small coal brazier used for warmth in the winter.

From the monthly poetry meeting at the home of the Master of Palace Repairs on the fifth day [of the Twelfth Month of 1451].

> Despite the depth
> of the snow
> > on Yodo Moor,
> there is still
> > a path—
> where a cart
> > sent off at dawn
> has left
> > its tracks behind.

♦ ♦ ♦ ♦ ♦

uzumedomo / yodono no yuki ni / michi zo aru /
akatsuki yarishi / oguruma no ato

138   *"First Autumn Wind"*

From the monthly poetry meeting at the home of the Master of Palace
Repairs on the fifth day [of the Twelfth Month of 1451].

> Ah, how I wish
> that I could feel
>   as I will later
> as winter's captive!
> It seems
>   too chilly, now—
> this first wind
>   of autumn.

♦ ♦ ♦ ♦ ♦

*nochi ni komu / fuyu no kokoro no / isogeba ya /
amari suzushiki / aki no hatsukaze*

"Regret for Blossoms"

From the monthly poetry meeting at the home of the Assistant Governor
of Kazusa on the sixth day [of the Third Month of 1452].

> The scattering
> of blossoms
>   in the wind
> lasts only a day—
> while we lament
>   the moon's
> descent
>   night
>   after night.

♦ ♦ ♦ ♦ ♦

*kaze ni chiru / hana o ichinichi ni / kagirikeru /
oshimarete iru / tsuki wa yona yona*

140   *"Blossoms at Dawn"*

Written extemporaneously* at the monthly poetry meeting at Myōeiji on
the fourteenth day [of the Third Month of 1452].

> Not like
>   the voices
> of birds
>   in the normal
>   world,
> those chirpings;
> but, then,
>   neither of this world
> is this dawn
>   of cherry blossoms.

✦ ✦ ✦ ✦ ✦

*yo no tsune no / tori no saezuru / koe narazu /
kono yo ni mo ninu / hana no akebono*

---

*In other words, composed on topics handed out "on the spot" rather than
beforehand.

From the monthly meeting at the home of the Master of the Right Capital
on the sixteenth day [of the Fifth Month of 1452].

> Onto the surface
> of the hard ore
> > of the earth
> white clouds
> > of heaven
> must have scattered
> > their seeds—
> now become blossoms
> > at their height.

♦ ♦ ♦ ♦ ♦

arakane no / tsuchi ni mo amatsu / shirakumo no /
tane wa arikeru / hanazakari kana

142   *"Buddhism, Related to 'the Moon'"*

From a sequence composed at the home of the Assistant Commander of the Military Guards of the Right on the seventeenth day [of the Seventh Month of 1452].

> "Look up!"
> someone says,
> pointing into
> empty sky
> with one finger—
> but no one
> bothers to obey
> and get
> a look
> at the moon.

♦ ♦ ♦ ♦ ♦

*aoge tote / munashiki sora ni / sasu yubi o /
mamorite tsuki o / miru hito mo nashi*

Written at the home of the Assistant Commander of the Military Guards of the Right on the eighteenth day [of the Eighth Month of 1452].

Growing old,
                    one
can forget completely
the recent
                    past—
although
                    remembering still
things from when
                    one was a child.

✦ ✦ ✦ ✦ ✦

oinureba / chikaki mukashi zo / wasuraruru /
itokenakarishi / koto wa oboete

144   *"Bridge in the Mist"*

Written while ill in bed when I did not want to postpone the monthly meeting at my cottage, on the twentieth day [of the Eighth Month of 1452].

Who can make it
                    over
the bridge
            on the mountain peak?
Even the morning mist
struggles
            to get across
in the wind
            below the clouds.

✦ ✦ ✦ ✦ ✦

tare koemu / mine no kakehashi / asagiri mo /
watariwazurau / kumo no shitakaze

"Faint Moonlight in the Mountains"

From the monthly poetry meeting at my cottage on the twentieth day [of the Ninth Month of 1452].

>Deep into
>>autumn,
>I hear
>>no mountain wind;
>in moonlight
>>spilling
>down
>>through gaps
>>>in the trees—
>the sound
>>of acorns
>>>hitting frost.

♦ ♦ ♦ ♦ ♦

aki fukaki / yamakaze kikade / ko no ma moru /
tsuki ni ochishii no / shimo o utsu koe

146   *"Feeling Far Away, in the Snow"*

A poem written on pocket paper* when there was a service held before a portrait of Teika at the home of the Master of Palace Repairs on the 29th day [of the Eleventh Month of 1452].

On
    Poetry Way
I stop
    the pony
        of my heart
for a brief
      rest—
thinking back
      on that snow
on the fields
     'round Sano Ford.†

✦ ✦ ✦ ✦ ✦

*yamatouta no / michi no kokoro no / koma tomete /
sano no watari no / yuki o shi zo omou*

* *Kaishi,* the paper upon which poems were written for gatherings and contests. The name derives from the custom of carrying the paper inside the breast pocket of one's robe.
†An allusive variation on *Shin kokinshū* 671, by Fujiwara no Teika (Travel): No shelter in sight / to give my pony a rest / and brush off my sleeves— / in the fields around Sano Ford / on a snowy evening. (koma tomete / sode uchiharau / kage mo nashi / sano no watari no / yuki no yūgure)

Written when people were composing poems at Ōmiya Jōkō'in on the
sixth day of the Twelfth Month [of 1452].

> I will not dry them—
> for might it not be
>   that someone
> from long ago
> has become
>   one
>   of these tears,
> now fallen
>   onto my sleeves?

✦ ✦ ✦ ✦ ✦

makihosaji / mukashi no hito ya / namida to mo /
narite tamoto ni / ima kakaruran

148   *"Hut of Grass"*

From the monthly poetry meeting at the home of the Master of Palace
Repairs on the eighteenth day [of the Twelfth Month of 1452].

And when
                my body
ends its brief stay
                and decays—
then the moss
                will age,
the grass
                of my rustic hut
becoming
                a memorial mound.

✦ ✦ ✦ ✦ ✦

kari ni sumu / mi mo kuchihateba / koke furite /
iori ya kusa no / tsuka to naramashi

From a poem sequence at the home of the Assistant Commander of the Military Guards of the Right on the 25th day [of the Twelfth Month of 1452].

> Frozen in channels
> among
>   rock crevasses,
> it must stay the night:
> for water, too,
>   a traveler's inn
> is a cold
>   place to sleep.

✦ ✦ ✦ ✦ ✦

kōriiru / iwama ni koyoi / todomarite /
mizu mo tabine no / yado ya samukeki

150   *"Pines on a Peak"*

From when the Ogasawara Bizen Lay-Monk Jōgan sponsored a monthly poetry meeting at a place called Myōeiji on the fourteenth day [of the First Month of 1453].

> Ah,
>   for the words
> to make
>   of that peak above
> overhung
>   with clouds
> a pine
>   at the mountain's base!
> The Way of Poetry.

✦ ✦ ✦ ✦ ✦

kumo kakaru / mine o fumoto no / matsu to nasu /
koto no ha mogana / shikishima no uta

Written for a votive sequence requested by a certain person on the 25th day [of the Second Month of 1453].

> Even
>   the clouds
> above
>   in the empty sky
> follow the wind.
> Who, then,
>   in this world
> avoids
>   submitting
>   to the Man?

+ + + + +

sora ni dani / kaze no mama naru / kumo zo aru /
hito ni shitagau / yo o ba somukaji

152   *"Love, Related to 'Bells'"*   ✓

From a poem sequence at the home of the Bizen Lay-Monk Jōgan at the
end of the Third Month [of 1453].

> As I listen,
> 　　　　　bells
> tolling over Hatsu River
> fade off,
> 　　　　　one by one—
> falling onto
> 　　　　　my sleeves,
> becoming
> 　　　　　the capital.*

✦ ✦ ✦ ✦ ✦

*kiku kane mo / koegoe taete / hatsusegawa /
sode ni ochikuru / miyako to zo naru*

*An allusion to *Shin kokinshū* 1142 (Love), by Fujiwara no Teika: The years
have gone by / with my prayers still unanswered— / as Hase's bell / signals evening
from its peak, / sounding somehow far away. (*toshi mo henu / inoru chigiri wa /
hatsuseyama / onoe no kane no / yoso no yugure*)

From the monthly poetry meeting at the home of the Master of Palace Repairs on the thirteenth day [of the Fourth Month of 1453].

> Yes,
>   the gods above
> have given us
>   treasured truths
> we should obey,
> but it is
>   the lies of men
> that stand out
>   in the world.

♦ ♦ ♦ ♦ ♦

mamoru beki / kami no makoto wa / arinagara /
hito no itsuwaru / yo zo shirushi naki

154   *"Willow on an Inlet"*

Composed extemporaneously for the monthly poetry meeting at my cottage on the twentieth day [of the Fifth Month of 1453].

> This
>   willow tree
> on the banks of the inlet—
> when
>   did it wither,
> leaving only
>   the pine trees
> as markers
>   of spring?

✦ ✦ ✦ ✦ ✦

kawakishi no / ōe no yanagi / itsu kuchite /
matsu bakari naru / haru no shirushi zo

Written for the monthly poetry meeting at Myōeiji on the fourteenth
day [of the Sixth Month of 1453].

> High up
>   on the peaks,
> those blotches
>   of black ink stuck
> to the sky's
>   deep blue—
> ah, they were only pine trees!
> On mountains,
>   in the evening.

+ + + + +

mine takaki / midori no sora ni / tsuku sumi wa /
matsu narikeri na / yūgure no yama

156   *"Mountain Home"*

From a seventy-poem sequence at the home of the Master of Palace Repairs on the seventh day [of the Seventh Month of 1453].

> Were I to emerge
> from the mountains
>   of Yoshino
> when my world
>   was gone,
> who then
>   would not mistake me
> for a man from China?

✦ ✦ ✦ ✦ ✦

sumu yo hete / yoshino no yama o / kari ni ideba / morokoshibito / to tare ka mizaran

From a hundred-poem sequence written extemporaneously for presentation as a votive offering for the Kitano Shrine made by Master of the Right Capital Haga Mototame on the twelfth day [of the Seventh Month of 1453].

Away
  they scattered
to gather up
   the fallen leaves—
village
  urchins.
But for shelter
   from showers
they are back
  beneath the evergreens.

♦ ♦ ♦ ♦ ♦

yoso ni shite / ochiba kakitoru / sato no ko mo /
shigure ni tanomu / tokiwagi no kage

158   *"Love, Related to 'Monkey'"*

From the monthly poetry meeting at Myōeiji on the nineteenth day [of the Eighth Month of 1453].

> The one
>   I glimpsed
> is just so
>   hard to catch—
> like
>   those monkeys
> vainly
>   stretching out
>   their hands
> for the moon
>   in a valley pool.*

♦ ♦ ♦ ♦ ♦

*mishi hito mo / kaku zo egataki / tani no saru /
te ni mo torarenu / mizu no tsukikage*

---

*A reference to an old Buddhist cautionary tale in which monkeys reach out for the image of the moon in a pool, fall in, and drown—symbolizing the fate that awaits all who are caught in the world of illusion.

From the monthly poetry meeting at my cottage on the twentieth day [of the Ninth Month of 1453].

> And if the rope
> does not reach
>
> down
>
> far enough
>
> into my heart,
> who will fathom
>
> the thoughts
>
> at the bottom
>
> of the well?

♦ ♦ ♦ ♦ ♦

tsurubenawa / kokoro fukai ni / oyobazu wa /
tare kumishiran / omou minasoko

160   *"Bell at a Traveler's Inn"*

From the monthly poetry meeting at Daikōmyōji on the twelfth day [of the Tenth Month of 1453].

> Listening,
>   I learn
>   that even
>   the night
>   is not like
>   what
>   I know at home;
>   even the bell
>   seems remote,
>   speaking with
>   a different voice.

✦ ✦ ✦ ✦ ✦

kiku mama ni / waga sato nareshi / yowa mo nizu /
kane sae hina no / koe zo kawareru

"Inn in Winter"

From the monthly poetry meeting of Enshū at Byōdōbō on the 25th day
[of the Eleventh Month of 1453].

> Across
>   a winter stream
> he fords,
>   as evening comes—
> going straight in
> to the fire tender's place,
> without even
>   asking
>   his name.

♦ ♦ ♦ ♦ ♦

fuyukawa o / yūwatari suru / hitakiya ni /
taga yado towade / mazu zo tachiiru

162   *"Evening Hail"*

From among the poems of a votive hundred-poem sequence composed at the home of the Assistant Commander of the Military Guards of the Right, as a prayer for my recovery from illness, on the fourth day of the Third Month [of 1454].

Storm clouds
　　　　　clear away;
then come blasts
　　　　　of icy wind,
scattering
　　　　hailstones—
looking
　　　as if
　　　　　the evening stars
were
　　　descending
　　　　　from the sky.

+ + + + +

sora harete / sayuru arashi ni / tama zo chiru /
yūbe no hoshi no / kudaru to ya min

From the monthly poetry meeting at the home of the Master of Palace Repairs on the fifth day of the Fifth Month [of 1454].

> To house
>   after house
> the woodcutter takes
>   bundles
> of wood
>   for burning,
> and then
>   turns for home
>   at dusk
> as the village
>   throbs
>   with sound.

✦ ✦ ✦ ✦ ✦

ieie ni / shiba mochiirite / yamabito no /
kaeru yūbe no / sato doyomu nari

164   *"Rain at Night in One's Home Town"*

From a poem sequence at the home of the Bizen Lay-Monk Jōgan on the 21st day [of the Sixth Month of 1454].

> All through the night
> rain
>   delivers
>   the voices
> of generations
> that have now become
>   these clouds
> spilling showers
>   on my hometown.

✦ ✦ ✦ ✦ ✦

yomosugara / koe o zo hakobu / yoyo no hito /
kumo to narinishi / furusato no ame

From a poem sequence at the home of the Assistant Commander of the Military Guards of the Right on the 27th day [of the Twelfth Month of 1454].

> Darkness has fallen.
> With my boat
> > > making no progress
> on Waka Bay,*
> I end this year
> > > as others,
> tossed on
> > > the waves
> > > > of old age.

✦ ✦ ✦ ✦ ✦

kurenikeri / waka no urabune / kogi sarazu / kotoshi mo oi no / nami ni ukabete

*Referring to a famous bay in Kii Province, but also to the "harbor" of Japanese Poetry (*waka*).

166   *"Beginning of Spring"*

On the night of the second day of the First Month of 1450, I had a dream in which there was a votive sequence for the gods at the home of Kamobe Yukimoto for which I was asked to produce the first poem, on the topic "Beginning of Spring," which I composed and then woke up. Bemused by the episode, I quickly wrote the poem down on a scrap of paper but said nothing about it to anyone. Then, in a dream on the 28th day of the Twelfth Month of 1454, Yukimoto summoned me for a votive sequence and said that the first poem, on the beginning of spring, should be just the one I had composed! So fascinated was I that the poems were identical that when I presented a votive sequence I used this "dream poem" as the first poem.

> At house after house
> they seem to be
>   awaiting
> the coming
>   of spring.
> In the garden,
>   late at night—
> doing
>   the morning cleaning.

✦ ✦ ✦ ✦ ✦

ieie ni / irikuru haru o / matsurame ya /
yofukaki niwa no / asakiyome shite

"Viewing Blossoms"

[From a votive sequence dating from 1455].

The days
pile up,
and I get used to them,
until
with
my eyes open
or with
my eyes closed,
still
the blossoms
appear.

✦ ✦ ✦ ✦ ✦

hi o kasane / narenishi nochi wa / me o hiraki /
me o tozuredomo / hana zo miekeru

168   *"Cooling Off Near a Well"*

From a poem sequence composed when some people came to his home on the eighth day [of the Intercalary Fourth Month of 1455].

> Has the water frozen?
> From a wellrope
>   hauled up
> from far below
> in
>   the depths
>   of summer—
> a cascade
>   of white jewels.

✦ ✦ ✦ ✦ ✦

kōreru ka / natsu mo fukai no / tsurubenawa /
kuriaguru mizu ni / otsuru shiratama

"Bell at an Old Temple"

From a poem sequence composed when some people came to my cottage on the eighth day [of the Intercalary Fourth Month of 1455].

> Ignoring its voice,
> how many
> > generations
> > > of men
>
> have grown old?
> Always the same
> > temple bells
> in the mountains
> > of the capital.

✦ ✦ ✦ ✦ ✦

kikisutete / iku yo no hito no / furinikemu /
onaji miyako no / yamadera no kane

170   *"Losing at Love"*

From the monthly poetry meeting at my cottage on the twentieth day [of the Sixth Month of 1455].

Too weary
           is my heart
to advance
           any further
on the way of love—
a horse
        not up
           to the race,
slowly being left
           behind.

✦ ✦ ✦ ✦ ✦

*koiji ni mo / susumu kokoro zo / yowariyuku /
kisoi no uma no / ato no ashinami*

From among the poems of an extemporaneous hundred-poem sequence composed at my cottage on 23d last, in celebration of the completion of the discussions of *The Tale of Genji* that I had been leading at the home of the Shogun for the past four years.

> Within
> > that
> > > body
> > whose lack of
> > > enlightenment
> > I blamed for my grief,
> > behold now
> > > how the flower
> > of the law
> > > has blossomed!

♦ ♦ ♦ ♦ ♦

satorienu / nageki no moto to / omoikoshi /
waga mi ni nori no / hana sakinikeri

172   *"Remaining Snow"*

From a meeting at the home of the Reizei Gentleman-in-Waiting Masatame on the 21st day [of the First Month of 1456].

> Fine flakes of snow
> melt
>   into
>   the empty sky—
> falling then
>   as dew,
> descending then
>   as drizzle,
> onto
>   a frozen garden.

+ + + + +

awayuki no / sora yori kiete / tsuyu to furi /
shizuku to ochite / kōru niwa kana

"Dream"

From the monthly poetry meeting of Enshū at Byōdōbō on the 28th day
[of the First Month of 1456].

> For those grown old
> both reality
>   and dreams
> are
>   within a dream
> that provides us
>   some diversion
> as we live on,
>   dawn to dusk.

✦ ✦ ✦ ✦ ✦

*oinureba / utsutsu mo yume mo / yume no uchi ni /
magirete akashi / kurasu bakari zo*

174   *"Forgotten Love"*

From a poem sequence at the home of the Director of the Imperial Stables
of the Right when the cherry blossoms in his garden were in full bloom,
on the 24th day [of the Second Month of 1456].

> I had forgotten—
> as I
>   kept on forgetting
> to remind
>   myself
> that those who vow to forget
> are the ones who can't forget.*

✦ ✦ ✦ ✦ ✦

*wasurekeri / wasuremu to omou / kokoro araba /
wasureji mono o / wasurehatetsutsu*

*An allusive variation on *Shūi gusō* (no. 268), the personal anthology of Fujiwara no
Teika: You've forgotten, you say? / All right, then, I too will forget / that when we
parted / I said I would convince myself / it was nothing but a dream. (wasurenu ya /
sa wa wasurekeri / waga kokoro / yume ni nase to zo / iite wakareshi)

From the monthly poetry meeting of Enshō at Byōdōbō on the 26th day [of the Third Month of 1456].

> Out ahead
>   of me
> I allow the same distance
> I have come
>   thus far,
> then
>   beneath the straight-up sun
> have my meal
>   of parched rice.

✦ ✦ ✦ ✦ ✦

koshi hodo no / michi o ba sue ni / nokoshiokite
katabukanu hi ni / mukau karemeshi

176   *"Geese Outside the Clouds"*

From among the poems of a votive hundred-poem sequence at the home
of the Assistant Commander of the Military Guards of the Right on the
ninth day [of the Fourth Month of 1456]

> With so vast
>   an array
> of different robes
>   of cloud,
> how can they manage?
> Those geese flying
>   in a row
> make only
>   a single sash.

✦ ✦ ✦ ✦ ✦

kazu shiranu / kumo no koromo ni / ikaga sen /
tsuranaru kari no / hitosuji no obi

"Mountain at Dusk"

From the monthly poetry meeting at my cottage on the twentieth day [of the Fifth Month of 1456].

> The hue
> of my heart
> as I lose myself in thought
> each evening
> recedes
> farther
> into the distance.
> With the mountain
> not moving.

✦ ✦ ✦ ✦ ✦

*omoiiru / kokoro no iro mo / kuregoto ni /
tōzakaru nari / yama wa ugokade*

178   *"Insects at Night"*

From the monthly poetry meeting of Enshū at Byōdōbō on the 24th day [of the Eighth Month of 1456].

> Before
>   it came out,
> the leaves
>   on the grasses
>   were thick
> with calling
>   insects
> that are sparsely
>   scattered now—
> chilled, it would seem,
>   by the moon.

✦ ✦ ✦ ✦ ✦

idenu ma wa / kusaba ni shigeku / naku mushi no /
mabara ni narinu / tsuki ya sayuran

From the monthly poetry meeting of Enshū at Byōdōbō on the 24th day
[of the Eighth Month of 1456].

> Even
>> the mountains
> all take
>> for themselves
>>> the form
> of
>> the first Buddha;
> and how ceaselessly
>>> the law
> is expounded
>> by storm winds.

✦ ✦ ✦ ✦ ✦

yama mo mina / moto no hotoke no / sugata nite
taezu minori o / toku arashi kana

180   *"Famous Market Town"*

Written while on my sickbed* for the monthly poetry meeting at my cot-
tage on the twentieth day [of the Ninth Month of 1456].

> They accumulate,
> but there
>   is no one
>   to buy them—
> these leaves
>   of words
> piling up
>   like wares
>   for sale
> beneath
>   the Sumiyoshi Pine.†

✦ ✦ ✦ ✦ ✦

*tsumoredomo / kau hito ya naki / sumiyoshi no /
hamabe no ichi no / matsu no koto no ha*

---

*He had been down since early in the month with his chronic ailment.
†Sumiyoshi was the site of a Shinto shrine in Settsu Province that was sacred
to poets.

"Buddhism"

From the monthly poetry meeting at my cottage on the twentieth day [of the Eleventh Month of 1456].

> Just
> > grasses, trees?
> Every living thing
> > > in life
> must borrow
> > > its form
> from the myriad
> > > of things
> a Buddha
> > can become.

✦ ✦ ✦ ✦ ✦

kusaki ka wa / iki to shi ikeru / mono wa mina /
hotoke no nareru / sugata o zo karu

182   *"Bridge"*

Written when there was a monthly poetry meeting to produce a votive
sequence to the god at the request of Tachibana Toyofumi, chief priest of
Takamatsu Daijingu, on the tenth day of the Second Month [of 1457].

> On
>   a long night,
> there is no guard
>   to bar the way
> on the bridge
>   of dreams;
> but those
>   who have grown old
> still labor to get across.

✦ ✦ ✦ ✦ ✦

nagaki yo no / yume no ukihashi / moru hito no /
naki ni mo oi zo / watariwazurau

On the morning of the fourteenth day [of the Second Month of 1457] my chronic ailment flared up, and by the 17th it looked like it might be the end. I wasn't even aware of the people who came to visit, but then, who knows why, I began to recover, little by little . . . and by the end of the Third Month I was somewhat better, when I received a message from the Master of Palace Repairs saying that there were still some blossoms left in his garden, that it would be a shame if I didn't see any at all this spring, and that I really should get outdoors, and so forth. So kind were his remonstrances, that I went . . . and looked at the blossoms. This was written for a fifty-poem sequence.

> This year
> > for springtime
> I stay
> > in the capital,
> but with my blinds down—
> blossoms deep in the mountains
> taking form
> > within my mind.

✦ ✦ ✦ ✦ ✦

kono haru wa / miyako nagara ni / tarekomete /
miyamazakura zo / omokage ni tatsu

184   *"Love, Related to 'Animal'"*

From an extemporaneous poetry meeting on the eighth day [of the Fourth Month of 1457], when Hōshun of the Myōkōji received an invitation from the Master of Palace Repairs.

Now that
              at last
the dogs
              that once barked at you
are
       used to your touch,
don't
         stay
                away from the house
they linger around
                     every night.

✦✦✦✦✦

togametsuru / inu mo tegai no / naru bakari /
yogoro tatazumu / yado na itoi so

From a votive poem contest at Takamatsu Daijingu on the tenth day [of the Fifth Month of 1457].

    Past and
           gone now
    is the time I awaited,
    leaving me
           clinging—
    anxious for wind
           from the pines,
    like dewdrops
           at break of day.

✦ ✦ ✦ ✦ ✦

tanomeshi wa / koro mo suginu o / matsukaze ni/
inochi kaketaru / akatsuki no tsuyu

186   *"Passing Like a Dream"*

From a poem sequence sponsored by the Ogasawara Bizen Lay-monk Jōgan at Myōeiji on the 29th day [of the Fifth Month of 1457].

> Whatever
>   one sees
> in the midst
>   of one's sleep
> ends
>   with waking;
> but the dreams
>   one has while awake
> sleeping
>   won't make you forget.

✦ ✦ ✦ ✦ ✦

nuru ga uchi ni / miru wa samuru o / kagiri nite /
samete no yume ni / nete mo wasurenu

From a poem sequence at the home of the Master of the Right Capital on the 21st day [of the Eight Month of 1457].

> All I'm asking
>   for
> is someone
>   living in these hills,
> wise about
>   the past.
> In
>   this same world,
>   after all,
> the moon—if awaited—
>   does appear.

✦ ✦ ✦ ✦ ✦

yama ni sumu / mukashi kashikoki / hito mogana / matarete izuru / tsuki mo aru yo ni

188   *"Dew in Autumn Paddies"*

From a monthly poetry meeting convened by Hinoshita Toshikage on the 25th day [of the Eighth Month of 1457].

Breaking
          a new field,
laboring peasants
                work up
a sweat
        —adding
to the numbers
                of dewdrops
on
    the heads
            of grain.

♦ ♦ ♦ ♦ ♦

arata yori / tami no kurushimu / ase ya nao /
kazu masaruran / ho no ue no tsuyu

From a poem contest at the Ontoku'in on the 23d day [of the Ninth Month of 1457].

> Hoisting
>   the sun
> after its light
>   had set—
> a ship's
>   white sail;
> and how bright
>   the hauling ropes
> of boatmen
>   in the offing.

✦ ✦ ✦ ✦ ✦

nokoru to mo / mienu irihi o / ho ni agete /
tsunade sayakeki / okitsu funabito

190   *"A Little Stream in the Fields"*

From the monthly poetry meeting at the home of the Master of Palace Repairs on the fifth day of the Eleventh Month [of 1457].

> It is
>   not a man,
> this stream
>   thinning to a trickle
> in the meadow;
> yet I
>   see wrinkles
>   of old age
> in the ripples
>   made by wind.

✦ ✦ ✦ ✦ ✦

hito naranu /nonaka no mizu no / yaseyuku ni /
oi no shiwa miru / kaze no sazanami

"Passing by a Market"

From the monthly poetry meeting at my cottage on the twentieth day [of the Eleventh Month of 1457].

> Moving on,
>   I go.
> In the makeshift
>   market stalls—
> everyone
>   has left;
> an evening crow
>   calls out above
> my pathway
>   beneath the trees.

♦ ♦ ♦ ♦ ♦

ware zo yuku / ichiba no kariya / hito taete /
yūgarasu naku / mori no shitamichi

192   *"Cold Trees"*

From the monthly poetry meeting at the home of the Master of Palace Repairs on the fifth day [of the Twelfth Month of 1457].

> Those blossoms,
> those leaves
> that will scatter
> later on,
> in the coming
> year—
> all are
> here now,
> in the branches
> on every
> winter-bound tree.

♦ ♦ ♦ ♦ ♦

kon toshi ni / chiru beki hodo no / hana mo ha mo /
ki goto no eda ni / komoru fuyu kana

From a votive hundred-poem sequence composed at the home of the Master of Palace Repairs on the sixteenth day [of the Twelfth Month of 1457].

One may
            break a bough
and adorn one's head with blossoms,
but they cannot conceal
that a flower
                is a flower
and old age
            is old age.

✦ ✦ ✦ ✦ ✦

yamazakura / orikazashite mo / hana wa hana /
oi wa oi to ya / kakure nakaran

194   *"Pledge of Love, in Autumn"*

From a seventy-poem sequence at the home of the Master of Palace Repairs on the seventh day [of the Seventh Month of 1458].

> Our pledge
> of love—
> is as the dew
> of evening
> hanging on grasses
> withered
> by the winds
> blowing
> at the far edge
> of autumn fields.

✦ ✦ ✦ ✦ ✦

uki naka no / chigiri wa aki no / suenokaze /
karuru kusaba nni / kakaru yūtsuyu

From the monthly poetry meeting of the Junior Assistant of the War
Ministry on the seventeenth day [of the Seventh Month of 1458].

> The bellsounds
>   have ceased;
> the wind, too,
>   makes
>   not a sound.
> For lodging, then,
> it will be
>   in evening's heart
> that my heart
>   takes refuge.

✦ ✦ ✦ ✦ ✦

kane mo tae / kaze mo oto senu / yūgure no /
kokoro ni yado o / karu kokoro kana

196   *"Love, Related to 'Stars'"*

From the monthly poetry meeting at my cottage on the twentieth day [of the Seventh Month of 1458].

For one
                    who doesn't come
I wait on,
                    wasting my time—
although
                    every night
the light of the stars,
                                    at least,
visits
          my bedchamber.

♦ ♦ ♦ ♦ ♦

konu hito o / matsu wa munashiku / akahoshi no /
kage wa yogoto ni / neya o toedomo

From a poem sequence composed the first time I went to the cottage of Chōdō'an Sōryū on the sixth day of the Eighth Month [of 1458].

> Has the new day dawned?
> On the beach
> > > of the inlet
> a horse
> > moves forward;
> a boat
> > pushes out, gets afloat—
> setting the village
> > > athrob.

✦ ✦ ✦ ✦ ✦

akenuru ka / irie no iso ni / uma susumi /
fune ideukabu / sato doyomu made

198   *"Birds Lodging in Evening Groves"*

From a poem sequence composed at the home of the Master of Palace
Repairs on the eighth day [of the Eighth Month of 1458].

> How moving
> > it is
> that birds
> > should quiet down
> in the groves
> > of trees,
> while still the village pulses
> in expectation
> > of night.

✦ ✦ ✦ ✦ ✦

*aware ni mo / tori no shizumaru / hayashi kana /
yūtodoroki no / sato wa nokorite*

With a hat
                of snow
and for a staff,
                    an icicle—
an aging pine,
leaning with the weight
                    of years
standing in
            a garden.

✦ ✦ ✦ ✦ ✦

kasa no yuki / tsurara no tsue o / tsuku matsu no /
oikatabukite / tateru niwa kana

200   *"A Boat Moving Away, Beyond the Haze"*

And
          on a day
when the whitecaps
                    in the wake
of a departing
                    boat
are obscured
                    by spreading haze—
to what
          does one compare
                    our world?*

＋ ＋ ＋ ＋ ＋

*yuku fune no / ato no shiranami / kasumu hi wa /
kono yo no naka o / nani ni tatoemu*

*An allusion to *Man'yōshū* 354, by Sami Mansei. See note on p. 97.

"Late Spring"

There is
        no place
it really comes from,
            no place
it returns to;
what can we be thinking,
           then,
to welcome spring,
          bid it farewell?

✦ ✦ ✦ ✦ ✦

kuru kata mo / kaeru tokoro mo / naki haru o /
okurimukau to / nani omouran

202   *"Lightning"*

In the dark
        of night,
with whom am I to share
the thoughts
        of my heart?
Suddenly
        the clouds blink—
a flash
     of autumn lightning.

♦ ♦ ♦ ♦ ♦

kuraki yo no / tare ni kokoro o / awasuran /
kumo zo matataku / aki no inazuma

On leaves
            fallen
around the bases
                    of the trees,
rainfall taps, asking,
"Where,
        since
                only yesterday,
can Autumn
            have gone off to?"

✦ ✦ ✦ ✦ ✦

ko no moto no / ochiba ga ue ni / otozurete /
kinō no aki o / tou shigure kana

204   *"Night Snow"*

The wind of night
for
        the space
                of a stride
grows suddenly calm:
from afar,
            I hear the sound
of branches
                breaking under snow.

✦ ✦ ✦ ✦ ✦

*sayokaze wa / tada hitoashi ni / shizumarite /
ochikata kikeba / yukiore no koe*

Like lance and shield
set to fend off
                    arrows shot
from a spindle-wood bow—
that is how ready
                    my heart is
to pursue
          the way of love.

♦ ♦ ♦ ♦ ♦

azusayumi / yasaki o fusegu / tatehoko to /
kokoro takaku mo / tanomu koi kana

206   *"Buddhism"*

Think of it
        not
as a place
        either perilous
or without peril—
this bridge
        across the expanse
Buddha extends
        for us
           to cross.

✦ ✦ ✦ ✦ ✦

ayauku mo / ayaukarazu mo / omou na yo /
watasu hotoke no / mama no tsugihashi

"A Thin Trail of Smoke Over a Mountain Dwelling"

The smoke
            rising
from a hut
            high on the peak—
I would see it
as a fishing line
                descending
from
        the River of Heaven.

✦ ✦ ✦ ✦ ✦

mine no io ni / tatsuru kemuri o / ama no kawa /
tsuri suru ito o / orosu to ya min

208   *"Buddhism"*

Seek though one may,
can one
      ever hope
           to meet him?
No,
    not even
where the Master
         of the Law*
hid himself
      on Vulture Peak.

♦ ♦ ♦ ♦ ♦

tazunete mo / aimimu mono ka / nori no shi no /
kakureshi washi no / yama ni ari tomo

*Referring to Shakyamuni, the historical Buddha.

Akamatsu Norisada. Precise dates unknown. Constable (*shugo*) of Tajima
  Province. (poems 120, 135)

Archbishop Kōkyō, d. 1433. Chief priest of Kai'inji. (poem 40)

Asakura Takakage, 1421–1481. Deputy to the Shiba family, constables of
  Echizen Province. (poem 188)

Ashikaga Yoshimasa, 1435–1490. Eighth of the Ashikaga shoguns and major
  patron of the arts. (poem 171)

Assistant Commander of the Military Guards of the Right—Shibukawa
  Yoshikane

Assistant Governor (*suke*) of Kazusa—Hosokawa Ujihisa

Assistant in the Board of Censors—Yamana Mochitoyo

Bishop Shinkei, 1406–1475. One of Shōtetsu's disciples; major linked verse
  poet. Head priest of the Jūjūshin'in. (poem 130)

Bizen Lay Monk Jōgan—Ogasawara Mochinaga

Bureau of Poetry. A government office where compilers of imperial
  anthologies and other documents stored materials and did their work.
  Located in the home of Reizei Tameyuki during Shōtetsu's time.

Butsuchi'in. A temple within the Miidera (formally known as Onjōji)
  complex on the southwestern shore of Lake Biwa.

Byōdōbō. A hermitage within the Kiyomizu Temple complex in the Eastern
  Hills of Kyoto.

Chōdō'an Sōryū. Identity unknown. (poem 197).

Chōsan. Precise dates unknown. Priest of Butsuchi'in. Judging from the
  regularity that his name appears in *Sōkonshū*, one of Shōtetsu's closest
  friends. (poems 109, 110, 112, 113)

Daikōmyōji. Family temple of the Fushimi imperial line, located in Fushimi.

Director of the Imperial Stables of the Right Mochizumi—Hatakeyama
  Mochizumi, Hosokawa Mochikata

Eisen'an. Location unknown.

Emperor Fushimi. 1265–1317. Major poet in his own right and patron of the arts. (poem 85)

Enshū. A monk associated with the Byōdōbō. (poems 161, 173, 175, 178, 179)

Fujiwara no Teika, 1162–1241. Founder of the medieval poetic tradition at court; worshiped by Shōtetsu as the one true god of poetry. (poem 146, 152, 174)

Fujiwara Toshinaga—Saitō Toshinaga

Gion Shrine. One of the most prominent of Shinto shrines. Located at the eastern end of Fourth Avenue in Kyoto. (poem 23)

Governor of Awa—Hatakeyama Yoshitada

Haga Mototame. Identity unknown. (poem 157)

Hasedera. Temple dedicated to the bodhisattva Kannon located in Yamato Province.

Hatakeyama Mochizumi, fl. ca. 1429–48. Also known by his Buddhist name Senku. Governor of Awa. One of Shōtetsu's most important patrons. (poems 35, 42, 46, 54, 55)

Hatakeyama Yoshitada, d. 1468. Also known by his Buddhist name, Kenryō. Governor of Awa Province; later Master of the Palace Repairs Office. One of Shōtetsu's primary patrons. (poems 33, 37, 38, 118, 131, 132, 133, 136, 137, 138, 146, 148, 153, 156, 163, 183, 184, 190, 192, 193, 194, 198)

Hatsusegawa. River with headwaters north of Hasedera that flows around the foot of Mount Miwa and across the Hira Plain near what is now Sakurai City.

Hie (also read Hiyoshi) Shrines. General name for a group of shrines located on the eastern slope of Mount Hiei, just northeast of the capital.

Hinoshita Toshikage—Asakura Takakage

Hōshōji. One of the six temples in the six-temple complex in the Shirakawa area. Founded by Emperor Shirakawa in 1077. (poem 46)

Hōshun. Priest of Myōkōji. (poem 184)

Hosokawa Dōkan—Hosokawa Mitsumoto

Hosokawa Katsumoto, 1430–1473. Grandson of Mitsumoto. Head of the Hosokawa clan and Shogunal Deputy three times, from 1445 to 1449, from 1452 to 64, and from 1468 until his death in 73. Became a formal student of Shōtetsu in 1450. (poems 141, 187)

Hosokawa Mitsumoto, 1378–1426. Also known as Gansei'in. Head of the

Hosokawa clan after his father's death in 1397. Shogunal Constable of Settsu, Tamba, Sanuki, and Tosa; Shogunal Deputy from 1412 to 1421. (poem 19)

Hosokawa Mochikata, 1403–1468. Also known as Dōken. Son of Mitsumoto. (poem 174)

Hosokawa Ujihisa. Son of Yorishige; official in War Ministry. (poem 139)

Ichijō Kaneyoshi, 1402–1481. Statesman-scholar who served three times as imperial regent. Major patron of the Reizei family, Shōtetsu, and many other poets. Author of the preface to *Sōkonshū*, Shōtetsu's personal anthology. (poem 51)

Ishiyama. Temple located near the southern tip of Lake Biwa.

Isonokami. Site of an old capital in Nara Prefecture.

Isshiki Norichika. d. 1451. Master of the Left Capital; Constable (*shugo*) of Ise and Tango provinces. (poems 50, 53, 111, 121, 129)

Ishō Tokugan. 1360–1437. Zen monk. (poem 3)

Izumi Shikibu, fl. ca. 970–1030. Lady-in-waiting to Empress Akiko and major poet. (poem 66)

Jōrakuji. Located in northern Kyoto, between First and Second Avenues on Aburakōji. Evidently site of monthly poetry meetings sponsored by Yamana Noriyuki.

Jūjūshin'in. A temple located south of Kiyomizudera in the Eastern Hills.

Junior Assistant of the War Ministry—Yamana Masakiyo

Kai'inji. A temple located in Nishioka.

Kamobe Yukimoto—Kogamo Yukimoto

Kasuga Shrine. Chief tutelary shrine of the Fujiwara family located just east of the old capital at Nara.

Kitano Shrine. Shrine dedicated to the memory of the Heian statesman-literatus Sugwara Michizane, located on the western outskirts of Kyoto.

Kiyomizudera. Large temple complex located on the southeastern outskirts of Kyoto.

Kogamo Yukimoto. A warrior in the service of Yamana Noriyuki (d. 1473). (poem 166)

Lord Ichijō—Ichijō Kaneyoshi

Master of Discipline Shinkei—Bishop Shinkei

Master of the Left Capital—Isshiki Norichika

Master of Palace Repairs—Hatakeyama Yoshitada

Master of the Palace Table Office—Takeda Nobukata

Master of the Right Capital—Hosokawa Mitsumoto, Hosokawa Katsumoto

Master of the Right Capital Haga Mototame—Haga Mototame

Minamoto no Michiteru. 1187–1248. Statesman-poet of the early thirteenth century.

Mochitoyo—Yamana Mochitoyo

Monk Jakuren, d. 1202. Major poet of the *Shin kokin* period.

Mount Hiei. Site of the Enryakuji temple complex, located in the mountains to the northeast of the capital. Headquarters of the Tendai sect of Buddhism.

Murasaki Shikibu. Lady-in-waiting to Empress Akiko and author of *The Tale of Genji*. (poem 8)

Mushiake Straits. Located in the Inland Sea, off the coast of Bizen.

Myōeiji. Precise location unknown.

Myōkōji. Precise location unknown.

Nihō Shōnin. Chief priest of Myōkōji.

Ninnaji. A temple of the Shingon sect located northwest of Kyoto.

Ogasawara Mochinaga. A shogunal officer who taught weaponry and horsemanship during the 1430s and 1440s. (poems 56, 119, 122, 150, 152, 164, 186)

Ōharano. A broad plain located on the western outskirts of Kyoto.

Ōhira Oki Lay Monk. Ōhira Sochin, from Tosa. (poem 39)

Ōmiya Jōkō'in. Location unknown. (poem 147)

Ono no Komachi, fl. ca. 850. Famous poet of the early classical period (poem 95)

Ontoku'in. Location unknown.

Reizei Gentleman-in-Waiting—Reizei Masatame

Reizei Masatame, 1445–1523. Son of Mochitame, grandson of Shōtetsu's teacher Tamemasa. (poem 172)

Reizei Tameyuki, d. 1439. Son of Shōtetsu's teacher, Reizei Tamemasa. (poem 34)

Reverend Ishō—Ishō Tokugan

Saitō Toshinaga, d. 1465. Chieftain of a powerful warrior clan in Mino Province.

Sami Mansei, early eighth century. (poem 200)

Sano Ford. An area beside the Ki River, southeast of Miwa Point, in Kii Province.

Senior Assistant in the Punishments Ministry—Akamatsu Norisada

Senior Assistant of the Central Affairs Ministry—Yamana Hirotaka

Shibukawa Yoshikane. Head of prominent warrior family. (poems 142, 143, 149, 162, 165, 176)

Shogun—Ashikaga Yoshimasa

Sōzei—Takayama Sōzei

Sumiyoshi Shrine. Located on Naniwa Bay in Settsu Province. Shrine to Sumiyoshi Myōjin, a patron god of poets.

Tachibana Toyofumi. Identity unknown. (poem 182)

Takamatsu Daijingu. Located in Kyoto near the intersection of Sanjō and Nishinotō'in.

Takasago. Coastal area in Harima Province noted for the beauty of its pines. Site of a famous Shinto Shrine.

Takayama Sōzei, d. 1455. A retainer of the Yamana clan who was one of Shōtetsu's poetic disciples; also an important linked verse poet. (poem 45)

Takeda Nobukata, 1420–1471. A prominent military leader; constable of Wakasa Province. (poem 117)

Tale of Genji, The. The most important of all classical tales, written in the early years of the eleventh century by Murasaki Shikibu. (poems 8, 171)

Tō Lay Monk of Shimōsa, Sokin—Tō no Ujikazu

Teika—Fujiwara no Teika

Tō no Ujikazu, d. 1471. A brother of the more famous Tsuneyori who was a disciple of Shōtetsu for a while. (poem 107)

Tonshōji. Temple located in Sanuki Province.

Tsukinowa Consultant Lay Monk Seishō—Tsukinowa Tadakata

Tsukinowa Tadakata. Middle Captain of the Left. (poem 127)

Vulture Peak. Gradhavakuta, the mountain in northern India where the historical Buddha expounded the teachings of the *Lotus Sutra*.

Waka Bay. Located at the mouth of the Ki River, in Kii Province.

Yamana Hirotaka, d. 1441. A member of the powerful Yamana clan and of one Shōtetsu's most prominent patrons. Murdered with the shogun Ashikaga Yoshinori in 1441. (poems 3, 44)

Yamana Masakiyo. Son of Norikiyo. Constable of Mimasaka and Iwami. (poem 195)

Yamana Mochitoyo, 1404–1473. Also known as Sōzen. One of the most powerful of fifteenth-century *daimyō*. (poems 45, 47)

Yodo Moor. The area around the confluence of the Uji, Kizu, and Katsura rivers.

Yoshino. Mountainous region in central and southern Yamato Province known for its rugged peaks, swift streams, cherry blossoms, and fall leaves. (poem 156)

SOURCES OF POEMS

Original texts of all the poems translated in this book can be found in volume 5 of *Shikashū taisei*, ed. Wakashū Kenkyūkai (Meiji Shoin, 1974). The numbers below correspond to the poems as numbered in that edition. Another version of *Sōkonshū*, in which the poems are organized strictly by topic rather than chronologically, is available in volume 8 of *Shimpen Kokka taikan* (Tokyo: Kadokawa Shoten, 1990).

Abbreviations:

E-5 *Eikyō gonen Shōtetsu eisō* (alternative title: *Shōgetsu Shōtetsu eisō*)
E-9 *Eikyō kunen Shōtetsu eisō*
TSU *Tsukikusa*
SO *Sōkonshū*

1. E-5: 11	16. TSU: 228	31. SO: 1055
2. E-5: 79	17. TSU: 288	32. SO: 1152
3. E-5: 98	18. TSU: 303	33. SO: 1194
4. E-5: 184	19. SO: 6	34. SO: 1202
5. E-9: 45	20. SO: 78	35. SO: 1392
6. E-9: 64	21. SO: 294	36. SO: 1649
7. E-9: 90	22. SO: 420	37. SO: 1657
8. E-9: 111	23. SO: 533	38. SO: 1658
9. TSU: 30	24. SO: 694	39. SO: 1742
10. TSU: 69	25. SO: 796	40. SO: 1758
11. TSU: 77	26. SO: 902	41. SO: 1895
12. TSU: 111	27. SO: 939	42. SO: 1954
13. TSU: 135	28. SO: 945	43. SO: 1974
14. TSU: 165	29. SO: 1028	44. SO: 2022
15. TSU: 226	30. SO: 1050	45. SO: 2044

46. SO: 2056	76. SO: 3868	106. SO: 5440
47. SO: 2240	77. SO: 3925	107. SO: 5443
48. SO: 2253	78. SO: 3928	108. SO: 5452
49. SO: 2372	79. SO: 3986	109. SO: 5455
50. SO: 2415	80. SO: 4047	110. SO: 5469
51. SO: 2469	81. SO: 4058	111. SO: 5516
52. SO: 2481	82. SO: 4109	112. SO: 5549
53. SO: 2492	83. SO: 4138	113. SO: 5554
54. SO: 2537	84. SO: 4177	114. SO: 5614
55. SO: 2538	85. SO: 4327	115. SO: 5625
56. SO: 2541	86. SO: 4443	116. SO: 5708
57. SO: 2736	87. SO: 4475	117. SO: 5805
58. SO: 2784	88. SO: 4626	118. SO: 5809
59. SO: 2915	89. SO: 4653	119. SO: 5989
60. SO: 2995	90. SO: 4829	120. SO: 5999
61. SO: 3028	91. SO: 4889	121. SO: 6027
62. SO: 3098	92. SO: 4935	122. SO: 6073
63. SO: 3142	93. SO: 4936	123. SO: 6152
64. SO: 3152	94. SO: 4937	124. SO: 6276
65. SO: 3170	95. SO: 4975	125. SO: 6332
66. SO: 3285	96. SO: 5010	126. SO: 6342
67. SO: 3299	97. SO: 5016	127. SO: 6365
68. SO: 3419	98. SO: 5038	128. SO: 6431
69. SO: 3444	99. SO: 5086	129. SO: 6578
70. SO: 3532	100. SO: 5116	130. SO: 6818
71. SO: 3583	101. SO: 5140	131. SO: 7005
72. SO: 3690	102. SO: 5169	132. SO: 7041
73. SO: 3713	103. SO: 5170	133. SO: 7061
74. SO: 3833	104. SO: 5275	134. SO: 7078
75. SO: 3859	105. SO: 5419	135. SO: 7130

136. so: 7171
137. so: 7176
138. so: 7179
139. so: 7433
140. so: 7440
141. so: 7521
142. so: 7622
143. so: 7656
144. so: 7685
145. so: 7697
146. so: 7804
147. so: 7817
148. so: 7823
149. so: 7861
150. so: 7884
151. so: 7956
152. so: 8014
153. so: 8026
154. so: 8069
155. so: 8102
156. so: 8135
157. so: 8147
158. so: 8241
159. so: 8268
160. so: 8305
161. so: 8362
162. so: 8443
163. so: 8541
164. so: 8593
165. so: 8743

166. so: 8813
167. so: 8814
168. so: 8900
169. so: 8902
170. so: 8988
171. so: 9075
172. so: 9258
173. so: 9268
174. so: 9291
175. so: 9362
176. so: 9387
177. so: 9435
178. so: 9494
179. so: 9495
180. so: 9549
181. so: 9594
182. so: 9698
183. so: 9720
184. so: 9741
185. so: 9774
186. so: 9810
187. so: 9907
188. so: 9913
189. so: 9980
190. so: 10043
191. so: 10071
192. so: 10085
193. so: 10120
194. so: 10452
195. so: 10471

196. so: 10479
197. so: 10483
198. so: 10487
199. so: 10602
200. so: 10756
201. so: 10814
202. so: 10959
203. so: 10970
204. so: 11000
205. so: 11074
206. so: 11191
207. so: 11233
208. so: 11236

INDEX OF FIRST LINES

All numbers are page numbers.

Translations from the Asian Classics

Major Plays of Chikamatsu, tr. Donald Keene 1961

Four Major Plays of Chikamatsu, tr. Donald Keene. Paperback ed. only.
  1961

*Records of the Grand Historian of China, translated from the Shih chi of
  Ssu-ma Ch'ien*, tr. Burton Watson, 2 vols. 1961

*Instructions for Practical Living and Other Neo-Confucian Writings by
  Wang Yang-ming*, tr. Wing-tsit Chan 1963

Chuang Tzu: Basic Writings, tr. Burton Watson, paperback ed. only. 1964

The Mahābhārata, tr. Chakravarthi V. Narasimhan. Also in paperback ed.
  1965

The Manyōshū, Nippon Gakujutsu Shinkōkai edition 1965

Su Tung-p'o: Selections from a Sung Dynasty Poet, tr. Burton Watson. Also
  in paperback ed. 1965

Bhartrihari: Poems, tr. Barbara Stoler Miller. Also in paperback ed. 1967

Basic Writings of Mo Tzu, Hsün Tzu, and Han Fei Tzu, tr. Burton Watson.
  Also in separate paperback eds. 1967

The Awakening of Faith, Attributed to Aśpvaghosha, tr. Yoshito S. Hakeda.
  Also in paperback ed. 1967

Reflections on Things at Hand: The Neo-Confucian Anthology, comp. Chu
  Hsi and Lü Tsu-ch'ien, tr. Wing-tsit Chan 1967

The Platform Sutra of the Sixth Patriarch, tr. Philip B. Yampolsky. Also in
  paperback ed. 1967

Essays in Idleness: The Tsurezuregusa of Kenkō, tr. Donald Keene. Also in
  paperback ed. 1967

The Pillow Book of Sei Shōnagon, tr. Ivan Morris, 2 vols. 1967

Two Plays of Ancient India: The Little Clay Cart and the Minister's Seal, tr.
  J. A. B. van Buitenen 1968

The Complete Works of Chuang Tzu, tr. Burton Watson 1968

The Romance of the Western Chamber (Hsi Hsiang chi), tr. S. I. Hsiung.
Also in paperback ed.   1968

The Manyōshū, Nippon Gakujutsu Shinkōkai edition. Paperback ed. only.
1969

Records of the Historian: Chapters from the Shih chi of Ssu-ma Ch'ien, tr.
Burton Watson. Paperback ed. only.   1969

Cold Mountain: 100 Poems by the T'ang Poet Han-shan, tr. Burton Watson.
Also in paperback ed.   1970

Twenty Plays of the Nō Theatre, ed. Donald Keene. Also in paperback ed.
1970

Chūshingura: The Treasury of Loyal Retainers, tr. Donald Keene. Also in
paperback ed.   1971

The Zen Master Hakuin: Selected Writings, tr. Philip B. Yampolsky   1971

*Chinese Rhyme-Prose: Poems in the Fu Form from the Han and Six
Dynasties Periods*, tr. Burton Watson. Also in paperback ed.   1971

Kūkai: Major Works, tr. Yoshito S. Hakeda. Also in paperback ed.   1972

*The Old Man Who Does as He Pleases: Selections from the Poetry and
Prose of Lu Yu*, tr. Burton Watson   1973

*The Lion's Roar of Queen Śrīmālā,*tr. Alex and Hideko Wayman   1974

*Courtier and Commoner in Ancient China: Selections from the History of
the Former Han by Pan Ku*, tr. Burton Watson. Also in paperback ed.
1974

*Japanese Literature in Chinese, vol. 1: Poetry and Prose in Chinese by
Japanese Writers of the Early Period*, tr. Burton Watson   1975

*Japanese Literature in Chinese, vol. 2: Poetry and Prose in Chinese by
Japanese Writers of the Later Period*, tr. Burton Watson   1976

Scripture of the Lotus Blossom of the Fine Dharma, tr. Leon Hurvitz. Also
in paperback ed.   1976

Love Song of the Dark Lord: Jayadeva's Gītagovinda, tr. Barbara Stoler
Miller. Also in paperback ed. Cloth ed. includes critical text of the
Sanskrit.   1977

Ryōkan: Zen Monk-Poet of Japan, tr. Burton Watson   1977

*Calming the Mind and Discerning the Real: From the Lam rim chen mo of
Tsoṇ-kha-pa*, tr. Alex Wayman   1978

Yoshitsune and the Thousand Cherry Trees: A Masterpiece of the Eighteenth-Century Japanese Puppet Theater, tr., annotated, and with introduction by Stanleigh H. Jones, Jr.   1993

The Lotus Sutra, tr. Burton Watson. Also in paperback ed.   1993

The Classic of Changes: A New Translation of the I Ching as Interpreted by Wang Bi, tr. Richard John Lynn   1994

Beyond Spring: Poems of the Sung Dynasty, tr. Julie Landau   1994

The Columbia Anthology of Traditional Chinese Literature, ed. Victor H. Mair   1994

Scenes for Mandarins: The Elite Theater of the Ming, tr. Cyril Birch   1995

Letters of Nichiren, ed. Philip B. Yampolsky; tr. Burton Watson et al.   1996

Sutra on the Expositions of Vimalakirti, tr. by Burton Watson   1997

Modern Asian Literature Series

Modern Japanese Drama: An Anthology, ed. and tr. Ted. Takaya. Also in paperback ed.   1979

Mask and Sword: Two Plays for the Contemporary Japanese Theater, by Yamazaki Masakazu, tr. J. Thomas Rimer   1980

Yokomitsu Riichi, Modernist, Dennis Keene   1980

Nepali Visions, Nepali Dreams: The Poetry of Laxmiprasad Devkota, tr. David Rubin   1980

Literature of the Hundred Flowers, vol. 1: Criticism and Polemics, ed. Hualing Nieh   1981

Literature of the Hundred Flowers, vol. 2: Poetry and Fiction, ed. Hualing Nieh   1981

Modern Chinese Stories and Novellas, 1919 1949, ed. Joseph S. M. Lau, C. T. Hsia, and Leo Ou-fan Lee. Also in paperback ed.   1984

A View by the Sea, by Yasuoka Shōtarō, tr. Kären Wigen Lewis   1984

Other Worlds; Arishima Takeo and the Bounds of Modern Japanese Fiction, by Paul Anderer   1984

Selected Poems of So Chongju, tr. with introduction by David R. McCann   1989

The Sting of Life: Four Contemporary Japanese Novelists, by Van C. Gessel   1989

Stories of Osaka Life, by Oda Sakunosuke, tr. Burton Watson   1990

The Bodhisattva, or Samantabhadra, by Ishikawa Jun, tr. with introduction
by William Jefferson Tyler   1990

The Travels of Lao Ts'an, by Liu T'ich-yunao, tr. Harold Shadick.
Morningside ed.   1990

Three Plays by Kōbō Abe, tr. with introduction by Donald Keene   1993

The Columbia Anthology of Modern Chinese Literature, ed. Joseph S. M.
Lau and Howard Goldblatt   1995

Modern Japanese Tanka, ed. and tr. by Makoto Ueda   1996

Studies in Asian Culture

1. *The Ōnin War: History of Its Origins and Background, with a Selective
Translation of the Chronicle of Ōnin,* by H. Paul Varley   1967

2. *Chinese Government in Ming Times: Seven Studies,* ed. Charles O.
Hucker   1969

3. *The Actors' Analects (Yakusha Rongo),* ed. and tr. by Charles J. Dunn and
Bungō Torigoe   1969

4. *Self and Society in Ming Thought,* by Wm. Theodore de Bary and the
Conference on Ming Thought. Also in paperback ed.   1970

5. *A History of Islamic Philosophy,* by Majid Fakhry, 2d ed.   1983

6. *Phantasies of a Love Thief: The Caurapañatcāśikā Attributed to Bilhaṇa,*
by Barbara Stoler Miller   1971

7. *Iqbal: Poet-Philosopher of Pakistan,* ed. Hafeez Malik   1971

8. *The Golden Tradition: An Anthology of Urdu Poetry,* ed. and tr. Ahmed
Ali. Also in paperback ed.   1973

9. *Conquerors and Confucians: Aspects of Political Change in Late Yüan
China,* by John W. Dardess   1973

10. *The Unfolding of Neo-Confucianism,* by Wm. Theodore de Bary and the
Conference on Seventeenth-Century Chinese Thought. Also in paper-
back ed.   1975

11. *To Acquire Wisdom: The Way of Wang Yang-ming,* by Julia Ching
1976

12. *Gods, Priests, and Warriors: The Bhṛgus of the Mahābhārata,* by Robert
P. Goldman   1977

13. *Mei Yao-ch'en and the Development of Early Sung Poetry,* by Jonathan Chaves   1976
14. *The Legend of Semimaru, Blind Musician of Japan,* by Susan Matisoff   1977
15. *Sir Sayyid Ahmad Khan and Muslim Modernization in India and Pakistan,* by Hafeez Malik   1980
16. *The Khilafat Movement: Religious Symbolism and Political Mobilization in India,* by Gail Minault   1982
17. *The World of K'ung Shang-jen: A Man of Letters in Early Ch'ing China,* by Richard Strassberg   1983
18. *The Lotus Boat: The Origins of Chinese Tz'u Poetry in T'ang Popular Culture,* by Marsha L. Wagner   1984
19. *Expressions of Self in Chinese Literature,* ed. Robert E. Hegel and Richard C. Hessney   1985
20. *Songs for the Bride: Women's Voices and Wedding Rites of Rural India,* by W. G. Archer; eds. Barbara Stoler Miller and Mildred Archer   1986
21. *A Heritage of Kings: One Man's Monarchy in the Confucian World,* by JaHyun Kim Haboush   1988

Companions to Asian Studies

Approaches to the Oriental Classics, ed. Wm. Theodore de Bary   1959
Early Chinese Literature, by Burton Watson. Also in paperback ed.   1962
Approaches to Asian Civilizations, eds. Wm. Theodore de Bary and Ainslie T. Embree   1964
The Classic Chinese Novel: A Critical Introduction, by C. T. Hsia. Also in paperback ed.   1968
Chinese Lyricism: Shih Poetry from the Second to the Twelfth Century, tr. Burton Watson. Also in paperback ed.   1971
A Syllabus of Indian Civilization, by Leonard A. Gordon and Barbara Stoler Miller   1971
Twentieth-Century Chinese Stories, ed. C. T. Hsia and Joseph S. M. Lau. Also in paperback ed.   1971
A Syllabus of Chinese Civilization, by J. Mason Gentzler, 2d ed.   1972
A Syllabus of Japanese Civilization, by H. Paul Varley, 2d ed.   1972

An Introduction to Chinese Civilization, ed. John Meskill, with the
 assistance of J. Mason Gentzler   1973
An Introduction to Japanese Civilization, ed. Arthur E. Tiedemann   1974
Ukifune: Love in the Tale of Genji, ed. Andrew Pekarik   1982
The Pleasures of Japanese Literature, by Donald Keene   1988
A Guide to Oriental Classics, eds. Wm. Theodore de Bary and Ainslie T.
 Embree; 3d edition ed. Amy Vladeck Heinrich, 2 vols.   1989

Introduction to Asian Civilizations
Wm. Theodore de Bary, Editor

Sources of Japanese Tradition, 1958; paperback ed., 2 vols., 1964
Sources of Indian Tradition, 1958; paperback ed., 2 vols., 1964; 2d ed., 2 vols.,
 1988
Sources of Chinese Tradition, 1960; paperback ed., 2 vols., 1964

Neo-Confucian Studies

*Instructions for Practical Living and Other Neo-Confucian Writings by
 Wang Yang-ming*, tr. Wing-tsit Chan   1963
Reflections on Things at Hand: The Neo-Confucian Anthology, comp.
 Chu Hsi and Lü Tsu-ch'ien, tr. Wing-tsit Chan   1967
Self and Society in Ming Thought, by Wm. Theodore de Bary and the
 Conference on Ming Thought. Also in paperback ed.   1970
The Unfolding of Neo-Confucianism, by Wm. Theodore de Bary and the
 Conference on Seventeenth-Century Chinese Thought. Also in paper-
 back ed.   1975
*Principle and Practicality: Essays in Neo-Confucianism and Practical
 Learning*, eds. Wm. Theodore de Bary and Irene Bloom. Also in paper-
 back ed.   1979
The Syncretic Religion of Lin Chao-en, by Judith A. Berling   1980
*The Renewal of Buddhism in China: Chu-hung and the Late Ming
 Synthesis*, by Chün-fang Yü   1981
Neo-Confucian Orthodoxy and the Learning of the Mind-and-Heart, by
 Wm. Theodore de Bary   1981

Yüan Thought: Chinese Thought and Religion Under the Mongols, eds.
Hok-lam Chan and Wm. Theodore de Bary   1982

The Liberal Tradition in China, by Wm. Theodore de Bary   1983

The Development and Decline of Chinese Cosmology, by John B.
Henderson   1984

The Rise of Neo-Confucianism in Korea, by Wm. Theodore de Bary and
JaHyun Kim Haboush   1985

Chiao Hung and the Restructuring of Neo-Confucianism in Late Ming, by
Edward T. Ch'ien   1985

Neo-Confucian Terms Explained: Pei-hsi tzu-i, by Ch'en Ch'un, ed. and
trans. Wing-tsit Chan   1986

Knowledge Painfully Acquired: K'un-chih chi, by Lo Ch'in-shun, ed. and
trans. Irene Bloom   1987

To Become a Sage: The Ten Diagrams on Sage Learning, by Yi T'oegye, ed.
and trans. Michael C. Kalton   1988

The Message of the Mind in Neo-Confucian Thought, by Wm. Theodore
de Bary   1989